THE AIRLINE INDUSTRY
AND THE
IMPACT OF DEREGULATION

Revised Edition

The Airline Industry and the Impact of Deregulation

Revised Edition

GEORGE WILLIAMS

First edition published 1993 by Ashgate Publishing Limited.
This revised edition published by
Avebury Aviation
Ashgate Publishing Limited
Gower House
Croft Road
Aldershot
Hants GU11 3HR
England

Ashgate Publishing Company
Old Post Road
Brookfield
Vermont 05036
USA

British Library Cataloguing in Publication Data

Williams, George
    Airline Industry and the Impact of Deregulation
    - 2Rev.ed.
    I. Title
    387.71
 ISBN 0 291 39824 3

Library of Congress Cataloging-in-Publication Data

Williams, George, 1948-
    The airline industry and the impact of deregulation /
    George Williams -- Rev.ed.
        p. cm.
    Includes index.
    ISBN 0-291-39824-3: $59.95 (US)
    1.Aeronautics, Commercial--United States--Deregulation.
    2. Airlines--United States--Deregulation. 3. Aeronautics,
    Commercial--Deregulation. 4. Competition, International.
    I. Title.
    HE9803.A4W53 1994
    387.7'1--dc20   94-27724
                                                             CIP

Printed in Great Britain at the University Press, Cambridge

Contents

List of tables

List of figures

Foreword

Stephen Wheatcroft

Director, Aviation and Tourism International

I was highly flattered by the invitation to write a Foreword for George Williams' first book. I knew and admired his work having been an external examiner for his Ph.D. at Cranfield. His dissertation impressed me because it was not only well researched but was one of the best written theses I have ever examined. I am very pleased that it is now being published as a book.

But I was a novice at Forewords. Consequently I turned for inspiration to the Foreword which Sir Peter Masefield wrote for my own first book - The Economics of European Air Transport - in 1956. I hope that I can be as helpful to George Williams as Peter Masefield was to me.

My revisit to The Economics of Air Transport led me to reflect on the astonishing changes in the air transport industry from 1956 to 1993. Technological changes are the most obvious: long range jet aircraft have transformed the world pattern of air services and enormously reduced the real costs of air travel. But the changes in the regulatory structure of the air transport industry have been no less remarkable, particularly in the last fourteen years since deregulation was set in motion in the United States.

This era of deregulation and liberalisation is covered by George Williams in a scholarly survey of developments in the industry since the passing of the US Airline Deregulation Act in 1978. His description and analysis of industry changes in the United States, Canada, Australia and Europe will long be invaluable reference sources for all those interested in these developments.

He describes the more gradual approach to airline deregulation in Europe and the Commission's determination that it will exercise a more effective control over mergers than the US has done. But gradualism in Europe has actually produced some remarkably rapid changes in the regulatory field and industry structure. We must remind ourselves that it is only six years since the Nouvelles Frontieres decision of the European Court of Justice put a bomb under the old system of restrictive bilateral regulation. In those six years the liberalisation process has been virtually completed. The 'Third Package' of liberalisation measures agreed by the Council of Ministers in 1992, which becomes effective on 1 January 1993, removes almost all previous restrictions on entry, capacity and pricing. By 1998 when the last remaining controls on cabotage are removed, air transport operations within the Community will be effectively deregulated and, if the proposed EC/EFTA agreement is concluded, an even wider area of free aviation trading will have been created. We have already seen the beginnings of cross-border investments and mergers which will radically change the structure of the airline industry in Europe now that harmonised rules for the issue of air operators certificates makes it more attractive to exercise the 'right of establishment' provided in the Treaty of Rome.

George Williams is rightly concerned about the preservation of competition in a deregulated airline industry. There is ample evidence that there are powerful pressures towards oligopolistic concentration in a deregulated airline regime. He proposes an intriguing antidote to these anti-competitive threats through a system of franchising route licences. Licences would come up for renewal and be tendered for every few years. The idea is worthy of debate though I do not, myself, think that it is a good solution. It is my view that competition will best be preserved by allowing greater freedom for the emerging megacarriers to compete in all markets. As a first step I would like to see a multilateral development in which all North American and European airlines could compete freely in a deregulated North American, North Atlantic and European market.

I think George Williams underestimates the irresistible pressures to change the structure of the world airline industry. Speaking of the European Community he says: 'It is difficult to envisage one of the more powerful Member States allowing its major carrier to be adversely affected by Community Policy'. But who in the airline world twenty years ago would have believed that any US government would have allowed Pan American to go bankrupt? And, nearer home, not many people thought in 1986 that British Airways would have a controlling interest in a German airline by 1993.

The impact of deregulation on the airline business is a fascinating subject and George Williams has made a splendid contribution to its further study. I commend this book to the whole industry.

Stephen Wheatcroft
Director, Aviation
& Tourism International

Introduction

Airline Deregulation has captured the interest of a wide audience not only because of its impact on large numbers of consumers, but also because the resulting transformed industry has borne increasingly less and less resemblance to the confident predictions of those that advocated the policy. Understanding the response of incumbent carriers to sudden economic freedom has provided a fascinatingly clear insight into the ways in which their managers have reacted to competition and more importantly, how they have sought to constrain the competitive process. Many of the surprises that economic deregulation of the scheduled airline industry has produced have stemmed from a considerable underestimation of the ingenuity of such individuals to devise and exploit means by which to protect what were to become their highly vulnerable markets. In many respects it is as if the industry had emerged from forty years captured in a regulatory time warp to replicate the type of strategic behaviour observed in other business sectors.

Whilst the markets for most goods and services have evolved over the past thirty years into internationally organised affairs, airline services continue to be held within a nationalistic framework despite their having played a key role in bringing about this re-orientation. That a person born, bred and resident in Scotland chooses to buy a Swedish car, use a refrigerator made in Italy, work in a Japanese owned factory selling the bulk of its production outside of Scotland, be influenced heavily in his/her purchasing habits by brand names strongly associated with particular countries and at the same time desire and be able to maintain a xenophobic national identity ironically seems to epitomise today's global marketplace. The basic need of each individual to have a national identity (of spatially manageable proportions with which the human mind can cope) has not been overrun by the internationalisation of markets. Where airline services are concerned however, territorial identity remains a crucial influencing factor.

1

Historically, in all regions of the globe, flag carrying scheduled airlines have played an important role in carrying their countries distinctive national characteristics abroad. Attitudes towards allowing this function to wane vary between governments. Those with large efficiently organised flag carriers have been happy to consign their airlines to international market forces in the certain knowledge of their firm's ability to survive and prosper at the expense of other less well endowed companies. For the latter group, deregulation is at best likely to consign them to performing subservient roles dictated by dominant consortia whilst a less optimistic forecast would envisage their total extinction.

In many respects it has been due to the strategic importance of aviation, partly the outcome of experiences gained during the second world war and partly stemming from the uncertainties engendered by the Cold War, that governments have been reluctant to relinquish tight control of this mode of transport. Although today most governments no longer would regard their flag carriers as performing as important a role as they once played in bringing their country to the world's attention, many still view their major airline as a form of national virility symbol. The desire to protect their own carrier's interests therefore has been, and remains, of paramount importance.

Accordingly, a key feature of the airline industry has been the strong bond with national identity, with most companies simply being known by the name of the country in which they are owned. This link continues to hold back and prevent the sector from evolving in a comparable manner and at a similar pace to most other areas of business activity. The presence throughout the world of foreign owned manufacturing plant and service industry outlets is commonplace and generally not regarded as intrusive or detrimental to national interests. This experience has yet to be accepted where airline services are concerned. The demise of a flag carrier or its acquisition and control by a foreign owned airline remains anathema. The disappearance of Pan American, long identified as the US flag carrier, has been allowed to go ahead by the US Government only in the certain knowledge that stronger nationally owned replacements have been ready to assume the mantle.

Where the airline industry is concerned, governments appear to want to hang on to the past. Vestiges of the days when territorial acquisition was the accepted means by which power was extended outside of one's national territory remain with it and continue to dog its development. That this outmoded colonial approach has been replaced in most parts of the industrially developed world with a more subtle means of extending a country's sphere of influence, one that avoids provoking retaliatory nationalistic feelings, appears to be ignored where this sector is concerned. Neither the takeover of home-owned companies nor the establishment of new business enterprises by foreigners provokes the degree of protectionism apparent in the airline industry. The perceived need to have the national flag paraded at major airports throughout the world appears curiously anachronistic when set against the tactics of today's economic invaders.

It is because the airline sector continues to retain these strong nationalistic affiliations that the deregulation of domestic scheduled airline services, whether in the US or elsewhere, cannot be regarded as providing a full and clear insight into how economic freedom will affect international operations. Privatisation will not radically alter this. Airlines will continue to be viewed by governments as useful assets to be manipulated in the furtherance of national policies. Only in so far as flag carrying airlines are superseded in these roles by other more efficient tools will the sector achieve the full evolutionary status of other industries.

1 Aims/expectations of airline deregulation

1.1 US Experience with Tight Economic Regulation

It was the Contract Air Mail Act of 1925 that enabled scheduled air transport services to become a permanent feature of the US scene for the first time. The Act introduced a system of contracts for the carriage of mail by air so providing the necessary stable financial environment for the development of such services. An amendment of the Act in 1930 gave considerable power to the Postmaster General who was able to use this to restructure the industry into a small number of trunk carriers operating transcontinental routes. However, the method used by the holder of this office to allocate air mail contracts was the subject of considerable controversy and resulted in a national scandal and the revocation of all existing contracts.[1] The Air Mail Act of 1934 was the outcome of this debacle and introduced a highly bureaucratic system of control involving no fewer than three separate regulatory bodies.[2] As Levine (1975) comments, given this dispersion of responsibilities carriers were able to abuse the system by submitting very low bids in the certain knowledge of having them later made profitable by the Interstate Commerce Commission. A number of fatal crashes in the three years following this Act led to strong pressure for the establishment of an organisation that was to be devoted exclusively to matters of air transport.

The Civil Aeronautics Authority (CAA) was set up in 1938 as a direct consequence of this and was given power to regulate pricing and entry on interstate routes, determine mail rates, and control all aspects of safety.[3] One of its first activities was to grant 'grandfather' rights[4] to the 23 carriers then in existence, who later became referred to as trunk carriers.[5] After the war these carriers faced competition from newly formed charter operators, who had been able to acquire aircraft and trained air crew at low cost. Charter services had been exempted from regulation by the CAA in 1938 and as a consequence operators were able to charge substantially lower fares than their scheduled counterparts. The trunk carriers reacted by introducing 'coach' fares, which as Davies (1972) shows had such a significant impact that by the end of the 1940s this class of traffic formed a large component of total demand. The Civil Aeronautics Board's reaction to this was to protect the scheduled carriers by attempting to restrict the operations of charter airlines, imposing limits on the number of flights they could undertake. A number of carriers managed to circumvent these restrictions by operating under a variety of different names, resulting in a higher provision of charter services than the regulatory authority had intended. Scheduled carriers could have responded to this competition by reducing prices, but the CAB was not enthusiastic about authorising low fares for such operations, a policy for which it was criticised by the US Senate in 1951.[6] In responding to this criticism the Board adopted a strategy of encouraging the trunk airlines to apply for coach fares, whilst simultaneously prohibiting charter operators from running anything remotely resembling a regular service. The dichotomy between scheduled and non-scheduled operations in US airline markets was thus established.

In a similar manner, CAB sought to protect the original 23 airlines by expanding its regulatory net to include the activities of cargo charter carriers who by then had started to make inroads to their markets. Indeed, apart from the approval of some Local Service airlines who were themselves strictly prevented from competing with trunk carriers, the authority maintained a complete ban on new entrants until the mid 1970s. It did however seek to increase the amount of non-price competition between scheduled carriers by licensing two or three trunk airlines on most city-pair markets. By 1970 of the top 135 city-pair markets, based on a combination of the top 100 ranked in terms of passenger numbers and the top 100 in terms of passenger-miles, ninety had two competitors and 38 had three.[7] CAB's stated objective in so doing was...'..to assure the sound development of an air transportation system properly adapted to the needs of the foreign and domestic commerce of the United States, of the Postal Service, and of the national defence.'[8]

Although by today's standards it seems ironic, the Board came under fierce criticism for this pro-competition policy. Bluestone (1953), for example, argued that the main result of attempting to introduce competition in this way had been to increase operating costs. On city-pairs with two or more licensed carriers, given an inability to vary prices competition had manifested itself in the form of increases in service frequency, resulting in lower load factors and higher unit costs. Profitability suffered as a consequence, leading to demands from the trunk carriers for higher fares. Fruhan (1972), using data from the mid 1960s, showed that load factor declined as the number of rivals on a route increased.[9] Figure 1.1 summarises his findings. Douglas (1971) using 1969 data for individual airlines in selected city-pairs confirmed this and showed a more pronounced downward trend in average load

6

factors than those indicated by Fruhan. By using a range of time valuations for travellers ($5-$10 per hour) Douglas had attempted to calculate optimum load factors on routes of differing length. Eads (1975) analysed these results and concluded that..'..during the late 1960s load factors were below optimal on all but relatively shorthaul monopoly routes.' This situation worsened considerably in the 1970s with carriers incurring substantial losses as a result of this and other forms of intense service rivalry.[10]

Figure 1.1   Load Factors by Trip Distance and Number of Rivals

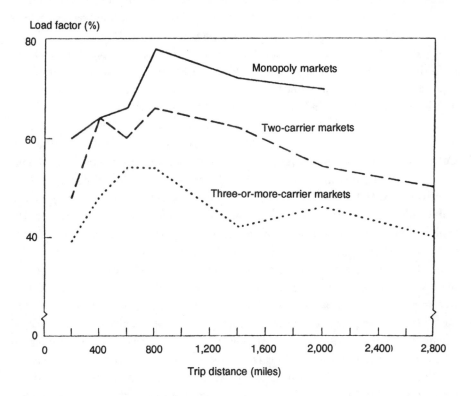

Source: Fruhan, W. E. (1972), The Fight for Competitive Advantage: A Study of the United States Domestic Trunk Air Carriers, Harvard University, Graduate School of Business Administration, p. 54.

One explanation for this was revealed by Taneja (1968) who modelled the relationship between a carrier's output and its market share in individual city-pair markets. The resulting S shaped relationship is now widely accepted and shows clearly that a unilateral decision by one carrier to reduce capacity on a route will result in a proportionally greater reduction in market share. Airlines faced with this situation according to Fruhan (1972) were placed in the familiar position of the 'prisoner's dilemma'[11], producing an outcome that none of them desired. Collusive action between carriers on a route could have resulted in an increase in average load factor, but this would have been only likely to have occurred under very stable market conditions. Eads (1975) attributes blame for this inefficiency on the CAB who through their willingness ..'..to grant fare increases when industry profits were low, regardless of evidence that the problem resulted from scheduling rivalry, has put the Board in a position of actually encouraging such rivalry.'

A policy of cross-subsidising short haul routes with long haul operations had also been pursued by the CAB. Eads (1975) shows this clearly in a graphical representation of unit costs and average yields by route length using 1965/6 data. This is reproduced below in figure 1.2. That fares were allowed to exceed costs by an increasing margin as route length increased above about 600 miles, enabled long haul services to operate at lower load factors, as is indicated in figure 1.1. Competition from ground transportation provides some explanation for this as Gronau's (1970) research into modal choice revealed. At distances up to approximately 600 miles, road and, in certain instances, rail transport provide a viable alternative to air travel.[12]   That this mileage coincides with the CAB's cross-subsidy boundary is entirely logical and confirms the regulator's primary preoccupation of ensuring adequate provision of services to small communities.

By the early 1970s the approach favoured by a majority of economists involved the dismantling of as many economic controls as possible, allowing market forces free rein. Kahn (1971) summarised the consensus viewpoint by pointing out ..'..that these cost-inflating service improvements have not been subjected to the test of having to compete with lower cost, lower service alternatives'. Attempting to eliminate the inefficiencies resulting from excessive service rivalry in any other way was fraught with difficulty. The Federal Aviation Act specifically prevented the CAB from constraining service frequency, whilst the other option of reducing the number of competitors on a route could realistically be achieved only through merger or the sale of a licence. To expect carriers of their own volition to agree to either of these courses of action required there to be a substantial commonality of interest. In the main, as Eads (1975) comments, this was unlikely to have been a realistic expectation.

Figure 1.2   Unit Costs and Average Yields by Route Length

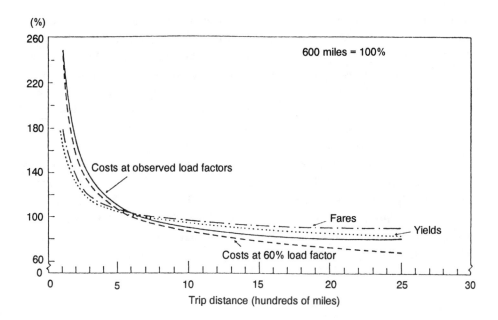

Source: Eads, G. C. (1975), 'Competition in the Domestic Trunk Airline Industry: Too Much Or Too Little?'; chapter 2 of Promoting Competition in Regulated Markets, edited by Almarin Phillips, The Brookings Institution, Washington, DC, p. 36.

Considerable weight was added to the deregulation cause from the experience gained in California of intrastate airline operations. On such routes the CAB had no jurisdiction, the controlling authority being the state's Public Utilities Commission whose only concern was in regulating price increases. As a consequence, airlines serving this market had been able to engage in price competition. The net impact of this was that over routes of comparable distance fares were considerably lower than on interstate city-pair markets. Jordan (1970) estimated that in the absence of regulation interstate trunk fares in 1965 would have been 32% to 47% lower than they actually were.[13] He had compared fares on Californian intrastate routes operated by Pacific Southwest Airlines (PSA) with CAB regulated trunk fares in the Northeast Corridor of the country. Problems of strict comparability arose however because of the congested nature of airline operations in the latter area. Jordan attributed the success of PSA, the then leading Californian intrastate carrier, to its low fare policy and greater efficiency, which he asserted were the outcome of less regulation.

It is worth exploring the PSA case as it provided protagonists with considerable evidence in support of their case for deregulation. That the airline's lower unit costs were derived from a number of sources is clear. A key factor had been their ability to employ non-unionised pilots on a mileage flown basis, whereas trunk carriers were severely constrained in this matter by section 401 of the Civil Aeronautics Act. Considerable economies could be achieved by concentrating on high density routes with common features. For example, PSA were able to use just one aircraft type configured for single class operation. In addition, by having the flexibility to vary fares, they were able to avoid matching the expensive service improvements of their trunk rivals. Given that all this had occurred as a result of having fewer economic constraints, it seemed reasonable to presume that this would be repeated in other markets if regulation was generally made less restrictive. That a large number of Californian intrastate airlines had failed was not regarded as being of any great consequence. Though trunk carriers had by comparison not been allowed to go under.[14]

1.2 Expectations of Deregulation Advocates

The overwhelming weight of evidence compiled by researchers during the 1960s convinced most observers that the CAB's primary preoccupation with protecting the airlines it had been given jurisdiction of in 1938, could no longer be regarded as being in the public interest. Forty years of tight regulation had resulted in an inefficient, stultified scheduled airline industry. A major concern of those regulating the industry had been to protect licence holders, with comparatively little regard being given to matters of efficiency or the interests of consumers. However, rather than pressing for a gradual change in the regulatory system, most interested parties favoured complete economic deregulation. The consequences of this decision forms the basis of the following chapter.

The fundamental and inevitable necessity for each carrier to provide its own protection against the competitive onslaught was given little, or no, serious consideration by those that advocated full scale economic deregulation. Entry barriers were perceived erroneously to be low, this judgement being based on observations of the small number of relatively non-regulated scheduled markets then existing. In the US it was widely anticipated that the overall effect of the passing of the Airline Deregulation Act would bear a close resemblance to that which had been experienced in the intrastate airline markets of California and Texas. The competitive pressures of these comparatively non-regulated markets had resulted in carriers such as Pacific Southwest and Southwest operating services at substantially lower cost than their regulated counterparts. This and the concomitant lower fares and wider range of services were expected to be replicated in the interstate markets. That the trunk airlines had had little scope or motive to change their operating environments, given the CAB's tight grip on the industry, and the fact that the likes of Pacific Southwest had posed no serious threat to them, would perhaps provide some explanation as to why these intrastate markets had remained so competitive. That this experience of low entry barriers was not reproduced on a national scale necessitates a careful analysis of the ways in which airlines, particularly the former trunk carriers, have responded to deregulation.

The clear expectation of those advocating total economic deregulation was that the sector would be transformed into a highly efficient, competitive and consumer orientated marketplace. Entry barriers would be negligible, so allowing new carriers to establish operations on any route they cared to choose. As a consequence, the high cost incumbent airlines would be forced to trim their expenses or be forced out of business. Fares would fall, in line with the improved operating economies. Small and medium sized carriers would be able to compete successfully with the then largest firms. That this idealistic vision was flawed was a result of the response of existing carriers to the real competition imposed upon them.

Notes

1. A detailed account of this period is provided by: Solberg, C. (1979), Conquest of the Skies: A History of Commercial Aviation in America, Little Brown & Co., Boston; and Davies, R. E. G. (1972), Airlines of the United States Since 1914, Smithsonian, Washington, DC.

2. The Post Office allocated contracts to the lowest bidders, but these rates could be adjusted later by the Interstate Commerce Commission to ensure profitability.

3. The Civil Aeronautics Authority changed its name to the Civil Aeronautics Board in 1940.

4. The term 'grandfather' rights in this context refers to the allocation of route licences.

5. By 1978 as a result of consolidation and merger this number had reduced to 11.

6. Bailey, E. E., Graham, D. R., & Kaplan, D. R. (1985), Deregulating the Airlines, MIT Press, Cambridge, Mass., pp. 18-20.

7. US Dept. of Transportation (1971), 'Top City Pairs, 1970'.
8. CAB 72 Stat. 740, 49 U.S.C. 1302(d).
9. In this Fruhan defines monopoly to mean 80% or more market share.
10. The introduction of wide-body aircraft was a key factor here.
11. The Prisoners' Dilemma game highlights the possibility of firms making gains from cooperation.
12. This applied to individual travellers; with groups a greater distance was revealed.
13. Load factors as a result were substantially higher for the intrastate airlines.
14. 14 out of 16 intrastate carriers had failed, whilst all 22 of the original trunks had survived, either intact or in a merged form.

Bibliography

Bluestone, D. W. (1953), 'The Problem of Competition Among Domestic Trunk Airlines - Part 1', Journal of Air Law and Commerce, Vol. 20.

Davies, R. E. G. (1972), Airlines of the United States Since 1914, Smithsonian, Washington, DC.

Douglas, G. W. (1971), 'Excess Capacity, Service Quality and the Structure of Airline Fares', Transportation Research Forum.

Eads, G. C. (1975), 'Competition in the Domestic Trunk Airline Industry: Too Much or Too Little?'; chapter 2 of Promoting Competition in Regulated Markets, edited by Almarin Phillips, The Brookings Institution, Washington, DC.

Fruhan, W. E. (1972), The Fight for Competitive Advantage: A Study of the United States Domestic Trunk Air Carriers, Harvard Graduate School of Business Administration, Division of Research, Boston, Mass..

Gronau, R. (1970), 'The Effect of Travelling Time on the Demand for Transportation', Journal of Political Economy, Vol. 78, pp. 377-94.

Jordan, W. A. (1970), Airline Regulation in America: Effects and Imperfections, The John Hopkins Press, Baltimore.

Kahn, A. E. (1971), The Economics of Regulation: Principles and Institutions Volume 2, John Wiley.

Levine, M. E. (1975), 'Regulating Airmail Transportation', Journal of Law and Economics, Vol. 18, No. 2, pp. 317-47.

Taneja, N. K. (1968), 'Airline Competition Analysis', Flight Transportation Laboratory Report R-68-2, Massachusetts Institute of Technology.

2 The response of US carriers

Back in 1978 few, if any, US airline executives had any realistic conception of how economic freedom was likely to affect their industry. This was hardly surprising given that the decision-making skills up to then required of them would bear little resemblance to those necessary to ensure survival in the competitive 'free for all' they were about to experience for the first time in over forty years. The policies pursued by the CAB had provided carriers with a high degree of protection from competition. Service frequency and in-flight facilities had provided the only scope for competitive rivalry.[1] All importantly, the need to provide their own protective barriers against competitive threats from existing and potential rivals in a dynamic and often unpredictable business environment, (something that managers working in industries not as tightly regulated would regard in the same vein as breathing) was a totally new phenomenon.

The CAB's strategy of segmenting the industry into trunk, local service and commuter operations with each carrier servicing its own respective markets, coupled with a highly restrictive route entry policy, had resulted in a high degree of interdependence between carriers. (Trunk carriers were certificated to operate long and medium haul interstate routes. Local service airlines originally operated to small and medium sized communities on low density routes, some of which were eligible for CAB subsidies to cover operating losses. In the 1960s many evolved from this feeder orientation to become medium sized companies operating jet aircraft. Commuter carriers provided service to very small communities and were exempt from CAB economic regulation. Strict limits were placed on the seating capacity and weight of aircraft that could be employed for such operations. From the late 1960s these carriers took over some of the operations of the local service airlines. Table 2.1 lists the trunk and local service airlines operating in 1978.) Most airlines were signatories to a multilateral agreement which required them to honour tickets issued by other participants.[2] As a consequence, immediately prior to deregulation approximately one in four US domestic passengers were interlining.[3] In addition to providing airlines with a highly stable operating environment, so enabling and at the same time necessitating this high degree of interdependence, the CAB's system of allocating route licences to trunk carriers had resulted in most of these companies having linear route networks. For example, Western's route map prior to deregulation, as depicted in figure 2.1, clearly shows the lack of a central hub. Once their protected status was removed these airlines, with their high operating costs and decentralised route systems, were particularly vulnerable to attack by low cost new entrants. An important early stage in the restructuring process following deregulation thus involved the trunk carriers re-orientating their route networks into hub and spoke systems. By 1983 Western had reconfigured its network routing much of its traffic via Salt Lake City, as shown in figure 2.2.

Table 2.1   Trunk and Local Service Airlines in 1978

Trunk Airlines	**Local Service Carriers**
American	Allegheny
Braniff	Frontier
Continental	Hughes Airwest
Delta	North Central
Eastern	Ozark
National	Piedmont
Northwest	Southern
Pan American	Texas International
TWA	
United	
Western	

A critical change that deregulation produced concerned the way in which passengers booked and acquired their tickets. Prior to 1978 the majority of passengers made their reservations direct with an airline. With the huge increase in options available to them, given the freedom of carriers to operate any route, travellers increasingly turned to travel agents for information and independent advice. It rapidly became imperative that incumbent carriers found some way to control this increasingly important point of sale. In fulfilment of this objective, the Computer Reservation System (CRS), employed previously as simply a cost saving devise to process large amounts of flight reservations data, proved of crucial importance. CRS owners had began installing their machines in travel agencies in 1975. Following the passing of the Deregulation Act, immediate access to flight information and seat availability rapidly became a priority for all travel agents. By prohibiting these agents from using other companies reservation systems and by varying commission payments, CRS owning airlines were able to regain control of the point of sale of their product.

In effect the CRS had undergone a metamorphosis to re-emerge as to what many now regard as the most successful airline marketing tool ever devised. The information collated by these systems enabled their owners to be most adept at targeting any response to a competitive challenge. The combination of a CRS and a carefully devised route network (based on the hub and spoke principle) has provided those companies so endowed with a degree of competitive advantage that has proved impossible to match by any other than those that are similarly equipped. A detailed examination of this feature of the deregulated airline market forms a significant part of this chapter.

Aside from making supposedly independent travel agents work to their advantage, airlines also sought to exert a more direct influence on the booking habits of regular travellers. Frequent flyer programs, providing regular travellers with free and upgraded trips, were introduced with the aim of capturing the loyalty of major users. The larger network operators were the main beneficiaries of this marketing strategy, as the rewards that they could offer their faithful clientele were much more attractive than those of airlines serving only a small number of destinations.

A number of other factors have played key roles in replacing the protective aspect of the operating environment that economic freedom removed. The rights of incumbent airlines to take-off and landing slots made it extremely difficult for new entrants to establish flight schedules at attractive times of the day.[4] The relative scarcity of peak hour slots has made them very valuable assets, taking them beyond the financial reach of many smaller airlines. Code-sharing alliances enabled carriers to extend their networks in cost-effective ways, whilst simultaneously neutralising a number of possible future competitors. More recently, major airlines have been acquiring their associated commuter carriers, with American being the first to create a nation-wide in-house network of feeder services.[5]

When taken together, the net impact of these various developments has been such as to provide positions of market dominance to a small number of very large carriers. The only other successful survivors of this period of rapid change are those that have been satisfying specific niche markets, such as Alaska and Southwest. Although other carriers are still in existence, for example, America West, they are in effect terminal cases simply awaiting their inevitable demise. Table 2.2 provides details of how the various new entrants to the interstate markets have fared since deregulation. The distribution of industry profits between carriers over the period 1987-1990 would tend to suggest that the industry is likely to undergo even further

15

market concentration. In 1988, for example, American, Delta, United and USAir accounted for some 86% of industry operating profits, whilst producing only 51% of the total volume of output supplied, measured in terms of Available Seat Kilometres (ASK's).

Table 2.2   New Interstate Market Entrants since Deregulation

Carrier	Year of Entry	Year of Exit	Reason for Exit
Former Intra-state Airlines			
Air California	1979	1987	Acquired by American
Air Florida	1979	1984	Bankruptcy
Pacific Southwest	1979	1987	Acquired by USAir
Southwest	1979		
Former Charter Airlines			
Capitol	1979	1984	Bankruptcy
World	1979	1985	Withdrew from scheduled services
Newly Formed Carriers			
Air Atlanta	1984	1987	Bankruptcy
Air One	1983	1984	Bankruptcy
American Intern'l	1982	1984	Bankruptcy
America West	1983		
Braniff	1984	1989	Bankruptcy
Florida Express	1984	1988	Acquired by Braniff
Hawaii Express	1982	1983	Bankruptcy
Jet America	1981	1987	Acquired by Alaska
MGM Grand	1987		
Midway	1979	1991	Bankruptcy
Midwest Express	1984		
Muse	1981	1985	Acquired by Southwest
Northeastern	1983	1985	Bankruptcy
Pacific East	1982	1984	Bankruptcy
Pacific Express	1982	1984	Bankruptcy
People Express	1981	1986	Acquired by Texas Air
Presidential	1985	1989	Bankruptcy
Regent Air	1985	1986	Bankruptcy

A detailed examination now follows of each of the issues raised above. Particular attention will be paid to their relative importance both in terms of the process of building immunity to competitive attack and in the subsequent exploitation of the market power resulting from this achievement.

Figure 2.1 Western's Route Map Prior to Deregulation

Figure 2.2 Western's Route Map After Deregulation

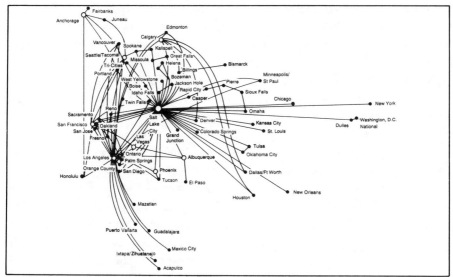

2.1   The Impact of Hub and Spoke Networks

The highly vulnerable nature of the linear route systems operated by the trunk airlines to competition was clearly demonstrated in the immediate period following the passing of the Deregulation Act. The more profitable high density city-pair markets were quickly targeted by both new entrants[6] and trunk operators. United, for example, embarked on a policy of vacating their lighter traffic routes in order to concentrate on such endeavours, selling off some of their smaller aircraft in the process. These more profitable routes were rapidly transformed into loss makers for the higher cost trunk carriers as fares tumbled.[7] It rapidly became apparent that to compete against lower cost and more efficiently organised new entrants necessitated a very different plan of campaign by the large established carriers. Developing a competitive advantage that would prove difficult to counter in this radically new environment became of paramount importance.

The first stage in this process involved these carriers redesigning their route systems into the now familiar hub and spoke configuration. By concentrating resources in this way airlines were able, through the better utilisation of their aircraft and flight crews, to derive considerable economies of density.[8] At the same time, economies of scope were obtained through the carriage of passengers with different origins or destinations on the same aircraft, resulting in 5-10% higher load factors on routes radiating from a hub.[9] The combined effect was such as to provide a level of service that rivals not operating from a hub found hard to match. Several of the former local service airlines already had developed networks based on this concept and so were well placed to enter the longer haul markets that deregulation made accessible. In addition, the smaller aircraft operated by these airlines enabled them to serve less dense city-pair markets more effectively by allowing a greater frequency of service than their larger rivals.

That this type of route system provided the most efficient way of overcoming the production indivisibilities inherent in the use of large aircraft is demonstrated in an engineering study by Kanafani (1981) into the relationship between aircraft technology and network structure. He examined the operation of a hypothetical commuter airline providing short haul services within a 500 km radius of Atlanta. When the results of this operation were compared with another more realistic airline system Kanafani found that...'... connectivity decreases with aircraft size and with a 140 seat aircraft the network reaches nearly a hub and spoke system.' This carrying capacity was the largest he considered, and it clearly shows that technically the best means of overcoming these indivibilities is to develop route systems based on the hub and spoke principle. An idea as to how large these production indivisibilities are is provided by Levine (1987) in an extensive paper dealing with US airline deregulation.

Such a regime allowed an airline equipped with aircraft of a given size to offer significantly more connections between cities than would have been possible by concentrating only on direct services.[10] The most effective way for the major carriers to turn this to their advantage therefore was by operating as comprehensive a route network as possible. In this way it became easier for operators with larger aircraft to compete in less dense markets, as raising the number of destinations served from a traffic hub enabled them to increase the size of aircraft and/or service frequency that could be operated to any one point in a network. The example given below provides a simple insight into this feature of the hub and spoke system.

Table 2.3 cites the case of an airline carrying traffic from town A to a hub at city B. If the number of locations that can be effectively served from A via B is set at three, then on the basis of the demand levels indicated it would be feasible to offer only three flights per day using a 30 seat commuter aircraft, such as the Saab 340. As the number of spokes from B is increased it is clear that aircraft size and/or service frequency can be raised, assuming that these locations are not better served via another traffic hub. Once it becomes feasible for the carrier based at B to fly jet aircraft to A, then even a long established local airline flying the route will become progressively less able to compete as the number of destinations the hub operator serves from B increases. In these circumstances a non-hub airline is likely to attract less traffic, necessitating the use of smaller, less appealing equipment.

Table 2.3   Example of a Carrier Operating to Hub B

Daily Flow	A-B	A-C	A-D	A-E	Total(A-B)
(for both directions)	20	40	10	30	100

(Assuming a 50% target load factor and three return services a day between A and B, the aircraft seating capacity required would be 33. If however a further six spokes were added to the network from B resulting in total traffic being attracted to travel between A and B reaching 250, then an aircraft seating around 85, such as a DC-9-10, would be warranted.)

As mentioned above, a number of the former local service airlines were at the outset of deregulation already operating hub and spoke networks. In addition, many of these regional carriers had developed their own feeder services, effectively reducing their reliance on the trunk airlines.[11] Given that many of them enjoyed significantly lower operating costs than their larger rivals, they were able to take advantage of their superior efficiency and, as a consequence, rapidly expand their operations.[12] The relative profitability of these former local service airlines in the years following deregulation has been critically dependent however on their ability to maintain a monopolistic position on the majority of their routes.[13]

The benefits of operating an exclusive route network is demonstrated clearly when comparisons are made between the experiences of Frontier and those of USAir (known as Allegheny until 1979). Despite having established well before the advent of deregulation an extensive hub and spoke network based on Denver, Frontier rapidly became unprofitable when Continental and United began to expand their operations there. Given their extensive national networks, passengers travelling via Denver were quickly attracted to the services of these two companies. That Frontier enjoyed a good reputation with consumers for service quality and had developed a strong market presence in the area was of little consequence in comparison to the network attractions of the two major airlines. The monopoly index devised by Toh and Higgins (1985) showed that by 1982 the former local service carrier was facing a considerable degree of competition in its markets, whilst by comparison USAir continued to have a virtual monopoly on many of the routes it operated from its Pittsburgh hub. The latter company's continuing concentration on short range operations, serving small and medium-sized locations, had been a crucial factor in it not being closely challenged by other carriers.[14] That other airlines were either not interested in developing operations at Pittsburgh or had been prevented from obtaining the necessary slots at constrained airports enabled USAir to remain profitable.[15]

It is apparent therefore that developing a coherent route network based on a central hub was only one of a number of conditions necessary for survival in the new era. Denver proved to be an attractive location for hub development to both Continental and United and it was undoubtedly this that led to Frontier's poor financial position and its ultimate acquisition in 1986. That its route network had lacked a central cohesiveness was only one factor in determining this outcome. Figure 2.3 reproduces Frontier's 1981 route system.

Some idea of the importance of traffic hubs is indicated by the extent and speed with which these developed. Prior to deregulation only Atlanta (Delta & Eastern), Chicago (United & American), Dallas (Braniff), Denver (United & Frontier), and New York (JFK) functioned as major traffic hubs. By 1987 however there were no less than 30 airports performing this role. Table 2.4 provides details of the proliferation of hubs between 1979 and 1988. An indication of the impact of this route restructuring on traffic flow is provided by Phillips (1987) who showed that between 1977 and 1984 whilst total domestic enplanements increased by 24% those at the major hubs had nearly doubled. (By convention a large hub is defined as one which attracts at least 1% of total domestic enplanements.) Table 2.5 lists the hubs developed by each major carrier in the decade following deregulation and shows the % of flights operated by each company from these locations,whilst table 2.6 shows the % of domestic enplanements carried by the dominant airline at each major hub.

Figure 2.3   **Frontier's 1981 Route System**

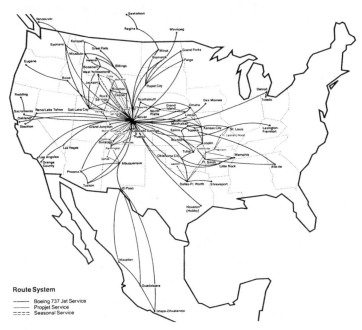

Table 2.4   **Proliferation of US Domestic Hubs**

Airport	Airlines Hubbing in 1979	Airlines Hubbing in 1988
Atlanta	Delta/Eastern	Delta/Eastern
Baltimore		Piedmont
Charlotte		Piedmont
Chicago (Midway)		Midway
Chicago (O'Hare)	American/United	United/American
Cincinnati		Delta
Dallas/FtWorth	American/Braniff	American/Delta
Dallas (Love)	Southwest	Southwest
Dayton		Piedmont
Denver	Frontier/United	United/Continental
Detroit		Northwest
Houston (Int)		Continental

21

Airport	Airlines Hubbing in 1979	Airlines Hubbing in 1988
LaGuardia		Eastern
Memphis		Northwest
Miami		Eastern
Minneapolis	Northwest	Northwest
Nashville		American
New York (JFK)		Pan Am/TWA
Newark		Continental
Philadelphia		USAir
Phoenix		America West
Pittsburgh	USAir	USAir
Raleigh-Durham		American
Salt Lake City		Delta
San Francisco	United	United
Seattle	United	United/Alaska
St Louis	TWA/Ozark	TWA
Washington (Dulles)		United

Sources: Treital, D. and Godly, M. (1988), 'Growing into New Hubs', Airline Business, September, p. 44; & Aviation Daily, Washington, DC, 14 April 1989, pp. 104-6.

Table 2.5   Hub Location and per cent of Flights Operated by Carrier

Airline	1978		1986		1988[#]	
American	Chicago	26	Dallas	42	Dallas	64
	Dallas	19	Chicago	28	Chicago	29
Continental	Denver	30	Houston	44	Houston	77
	Los Angeles	14	Denver	36	Denver	43
					Newark	43
Delta	Atlanta	35	Atlanta	42	Atlanta	58
	Chicago	9	Dallas	16	Salt Lake	79
					Dallas	26
Eastern	Atlanta	34	Atlanta	41	Miami	45
	Miami	11	Miami	10	Atlanta	36
Northwest	Minneapolis	30	Minneapolis	36	Minn'lis	78
	Chicago	23	Detroit	13	Detroit	59
					Memphis	84
TWA	Chicago	25	St Louis	60	St Louis	83

Airline	1978		1986		1988#	
	St Louis	19	JFK	17	JFK	28
United	Chicago	27	Chicago	35	Chicago	51
	San Fran'co	13	Denver	16	Denver	44
					San F'co	40
					Seattle	31
USAir	Pittsburgh	26	Pittsburgh	46	Pittsburgh	85
	Philadelphia	18	Philadelphia	17	Phil'phia	37
Western	Los Angeles	33	Salt Lake	49		
	Las Vegas	16	Los Angeles	23		

(# - First six months. 1988 data refers to enplanements.)

Sources: Aviation Daily, Washington, DC, 14 April 1989, pp. 104-6; & Jenks, C. (1986), 'US Airlines Hubs and Spokes', Travel & Tourism Analyst, August, p. 30.

Table 2.6   Per cent Enplanements by Dominant Carriers at Major Hubs

Hub	1977		1984		1990	
Chicago (O'Hare)	United	30	United	46	United	49
Atlanta	Delta	50	Delta	52	Delta	57
Dallas-Ft Worth	Braniff	34	American	61	American	63
Los Angeles	United	28	United	22	United	18
Denver	United	32	United	40	United	49
Newark	Eastern	30	People Ex	50	Continental	48
San Francisco	United	42	United	37	United	39
La Guardia	Eastern	31	Eastern	32	USAir	16
Boston	Eastern	24	Eastern	22	USAir	18
St Louis	TWA	40	TWA	58	TWA	79
JFK	American	18	TWA	21	TWA	31
Washington (Nat)	Eastern	28	Eastern	24	USAir	21
Pittsburgh	USAir	46	USAir	77	USAir	87
Minneapolis	Northwest	46	Northwest	47	Northwest	80
Phoenix	American	27	Republic	19	America West	46
Miami	Eastern	38	Eastern	47	American	20
Houston (Int)	Continental	37	Continental	45	Continental	77
Detroit	Delta	21	Republic	29	Northwest	69
Seattle	United	32	United	28	United	23
Las Vegas	Western	27	United	16	America West	39
Philadelphia	USAir	22	USAir	24	USAir	46

Hub	1977		1984		1990	
Charlotte			Piedmont	74	USAir	93
Orlando			Eastern	27	Delta	31
Tampa	Eastern	31	Delta	23	USAir	28
San Diego			PSA	26	USAir	19
Salt Lake City			Western	71	Delta	84

Sources: Phillips, L. T. (1985), 'Structural Change in the Airline Industry: Carrier Concentration at Large Hub Airports and Its Implications for Competitive Behaviour', Transportation Journal, Winter, p. 24; & Aviation Daily, Washington, DC, 14 April 1989, pp. 104-6 & 16 August 1991, pp. 318-20.)

Table 2.7 lists the domestic traffic share of carriers at major US airports in 1990. As is apparent, it is the busiest airports with over 20 million enplanements a year that have been able to support two hub carriers, notably Chicago, Atlanta and Dallas. The only other airports used as hubs by two carriers, Denver and Phoenix, in each case account for only about 50% of the domestic traffic throughput at each of the above three. At the time of writing, America West based in Phoenix is operating under Chapter 11 bankruptcy protection and has been experiencing strong competitive pressure from Southwest. The former's longer term survival as a separate entity would appear remote. (Further information about this carrier is contained in Appendix 1.) All other medium sized airports support just one hub operator.

Table 2.7   Domestic Market Share at Major Airports in 1990

Airport	Total Enplanements(mn)	Carrier(s)	%Traffic
Chicago	24.32	United	49
(O'Hare)		American	34
Atlanta	21.93	Delta	57
		Eastern	36
Dallas	21.73	American	63
(DFW)		Delta	30
Los Angeles	16.79	United	18
		Delta	16
		American	16
		USAir	13
San Francisco	12.47	United	39

Airport	Enplanements(mn)	Carrier(s)	%Traffic
		USAir	14
Denver	11.84	United	49
		Continental	34
Phoenix	10.68	America West	46
		Southwest	22
La Guardia	10.34	USAir	16
		Delta	13
		Eastern	13
		American	12
		Pan Am	11
Newark	9.27	Continental	48
		USAir	12
		United	11
		American	11
Detroit	9.22	Northwest	69
St. Louis	9.17	TWA	79
Boston	8.81	USAir	18
		Delta	17
		American	12
		Northwest	11
Minneapolis	8.43	Northwest	80
Pittsburgh	7.76	USAir	87
Las Vegas	7.62	America West	39
		Southwest	13
		American	11
Orlando	7.45	Delta	31
		USAir	18
Miami	7.01	American	20
		Pan Am	17
		Eastern	17
		USAir	16
Charlotte	6.98	USAir	93
Washington	6.95	USAir	21
(National)		Eastern	12
		Northwest	10
Seattle	6.86	United	23
		Alaska	22
		Northwest	13

Airport	Enplanements(mn)	Carrier(s)	%Traffic
		Delta	10
Houston (Intercont)	6.85	Continental	77
Philadelphia	6.73	USAir	46
		Midway	11
New York (JFK)	5.72	TWA	31
		Pan Am	27
		American	24
San Diego	5.21	USAir	19
		Southwest	17
		American	14
		United	12
		America West	11
		Delta	10
Salt Lake City	5.08	Delta	84
Tampa	4.71	USAir	28
		Delta	17
		Eastern	11
Baltimore	4.27	USAir	68
Raleigh	4.26	American	79
Washington (Dulles)	4.14	United	65
		American	10

Source: Aviation Daily, 16 August 1991, pp. 318-20.

To maximise interchange potential ideally a hub needs to be located along one of the main traffic flows (Figure 2.4 shows the main traffic flows across the country and indicates the location of each hub). Large traffic generating/attracting centres theoretically provide the best proposition, but often these have had limitations on the amount of airport infrastructure available so constraining development. To help overcome this problem competing hubs were established in the later part of the 1980s at locations with low volumes of local traffic but with plenty of space for expansion. In this way carriers were able to access traffic previously denied them by limitations placed on them at major congested airports.

Airports located on the eastern and western seaboards have not, in the main, emerged as major traffic hubs, the two exceptions are Newark and San Francisco. At the former, Continental has the largest domestic traffic hub in the northeast of the country. It had been developed originally by People Express in the early/mid 1980s, but became part of Continental's operations in 1987 when the carrier was acquired by Texas Air Corporation. Given that opportunities for domestic interlining are limited to north-south routings at a coastal traffic hub, the rationale for such a strategy rests on one or other of two possibilities. Either the hub can function as a feed point for international services or, if the location is at one of the country's main traffic generating and attracting centres with limited airport infrastructure, it can function in a purely domestic capacity. Ideally the two functions would be combined, as is the case with United at San Francisco. At New York the crucial requirement of being able to feed an international network of routes efficiently has been clearly demonstrated by the failings of Pan Am and TWA. In both cases the primary focal points of their domestic operations, Miami in the case of Pan Am and St. Louis in respect of TWA, did not coincide with that of their trans-Atlantic services mostly radiating from JFK.

Figure 2.4   Main US Traffic Flows and Hub Locations

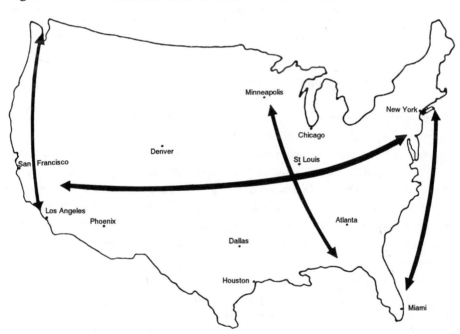

To provide a comprehensive network of services throughout the US carriers needed to have more than one hub. A good deal of hub development and expansion in the mid and late 1980s was achieved through merger and acquisition, which often appeared a more attractive option than slogging it out with competitors. The background to the governmental approval of this move toward greater market concentration and the implications of this for competition are discussed in detail in chapter 3.

It is apparent that the hub and spoke system of operating a network of services became the first means by which established carriers were able to protect their markets. The commonality of interest that the era of tight regulation had produced in which carriers had been forced to be mutually reliant in supplying each other with feeder traffic was quickly replaced by a situation in which it was imperative for each carrier to be as self-reliant as possible. A hub and spoke system reduced the scale of this dependency, simultaneously providing a degree of protection from would-be interlopers. Carriers offering only a point to point service would, all other things being equal, achieve lower load factors than an airline operating the same route from a hub. Unless the former had significantly lower operating costs, or had some means of successfully differentiating its product, it would therefore operate at a relative disadvantage to the latter.[16] This first and necessary step in the path to developing a sustainable competitive advantage, although being an important distinguishing characteristic of those that have survived economic freedom, of itself did not guarantee survival.

2.2   The Impact of Computer Reservation Systems

To argue that the Computer Reservation System (CRS) has had a significant impact in determining the structure of the deregulated airline industry is to understate its importance. This amazing adaptation of computer technology has played a crucial role in enabling a small number of carriers to achieve positions of market dominance. An in-house CRS has provided airline managers with a degree of clarity about the demand for their various offerings that one would ordinarily only associate with the hypothetical examples contained in elementary microeconomics textbooks. Indeed, given the existence of independently owned CRSs it is highly probable that the restructured airline industry would exhibit far less market concentration than it does today. There can be few industries that are characterised by the ability of a number, but not all, of their largest firms to control the sale of their products through retail outlets that they do not own, whilst simultaneously getting their rivals to be so dependent that they have little choice but to supply them with what normally would be regarded as highly confidential information.

The objectives of those first involved in developing the CRS were fairly innocuous. American initiated this activity in the late 1950s when it set out to establish a real-time data processing system which would enable it to access the flight details of any of its passengers at all of the company's locations. It took IBM

28

and American six years to perfect Sabre (Semi-Automated Business Research Environment), with the system coming on stream in 1964. TWA and United were quick to follow in developing their own systems, which at this stage were regarded by all involved as purely labour and time saving devices for handling large and growing amounts of reservations data. A number of attempts were made during the late 1960s and 1970s to develop a single industry-wide system with the aim of minimising unnecessary duplication, but all proved unsuccessful. One such system, Marsplus, remained active for several years servicing some 300 agencies. Some of the background to these 'neutral' proposals are provided by Feldman (1987), who remarks with some irony that one of the reasons for their failure was ..'fear of the government's suspicions that a joint system would be anti-competitive'. A public commitment by both American and United that they would make their systems available to travel agents made the huge investment necessary to establish an additional independent CRS even less of an attractive proposition.

As will be made clear below, airlines subsequently have been able to derive substantial incremental revenues by biassing information display and adopting incentive commission packages that reward travel agents for abandoning their impartiality, whereas a non-airline owned system would had to have relied exclusively on fees received from agents and airlines. Pre 1978, tight regulation and the concomitant high degree of airline interdependence precluded anyone from thinking that of itself the ability to access such large amounts of data could render a position of considerable power.

United became the first carrier to install a CRS in a travel agency in 1975. It was quickly overtaken by American who, within a year, had signed up 90 of the top 100 companies.[17] At this stage agents paid directly for this automated service, with each receiving an identical amount of sale's commission irrespective of which carrier's flights were booked.[18] This ostensibly benign approach to the use of the new technology quickly became transformed into one displaying considerable self-interest once the previously secure markets of the larger carriers began to be eroded.

Following deregulation the number of options facing travellers in terms of their choice of carrier, routing and fare increased beyond all recognition. Passengers could no longer rely on individual airlines to provide them with a comprehensive listing of the alternatives available to them. Their only reliable and seemingly independent way of accessing this information involved them using the services of travel agents. How essential a piece of equipment the CRS became to the travel agency industry is shown by the information contained in table 2.8. Within a decade, such a transformation had occurred that by the mid 1980s all but a small minority of agencies were equipped with a CRS.

Table 2.8   Number of Travel Agents and per cent Equipped with CRS

Year	No. of Agents	% with CRS
1977	13454	5
1979	16112	24
1981	19203	59
1983	23059	85
1985	27193	90
1987	29370	95

Source: Feldman, J. (1987), 'CRS in the USA', Travel & Tourism Analyst, September, p. 5.

The removal of constraints on route entry and fares resulted in a considerable change in the way passengers both accessed information about flights and subsequently booked them. Prior to deregulation around two thirds of bookings were made direct with airlines, but by the mid 1980s some 80% were being made via travel agencies.[19] Although the total number of agencies has substantially increased as a result of this, to a large extent this gives a misleading impression of how this particular market has changed. As is the case in many industries, a relatively small number of companies still account for a large % of the total sales. Wardell (1987) estimated that in 1985 over 37% of sales were accounted for by fewer than 4% of agencies. (Table 2.9 reproduces his analysis of sales volumes for the US travel agency business in 1985.) CRS vendors therefore have had a great deal to gain by extracting exclusive contractual agreements from the larger agencies.

Table 2.9   US Travel Agencies in 1985

Volume of Sales	No. of Agencies	% of Total	% of Sales
<$5m	20427	96.5	62.3
$5-15m	587	2.8	15.3
$15-40m	111	0.5	8.1
>$40m	42	0.2	14.3

Source: Wardell, D. (1987), 'Airline Reservation Systems in the USA', Travel & Tourism Analyst, January, p. 52.

In the first few years following the introduction of the CRS to travel agencies, airlines naturally concentrated on locating their equipment in the geographic regions in which they operated most of their services. In order to obtain a wider coverage some CRS owners entered into reciprocal agreements with other airlines to make use of their machines in areas where they had only a minor market presence. With restrictions on route entry lifted however, airlines quickly expanded their networks and this arrangement was superseded by one in which each of the major CRS owners found it desirable to install their own equipment with as many agencies as possible. At first some agents adopted more than one system, but this practice was swiftly halted by airline owners, who by supplying CRS equipment to agents at little or no cost were able to persuade retailers to sign exclusive contracts with them. As Levine (1987) has remarked, this made good commercial sense to both parties as ...'The agency enjoyed the benefits of automation at prices deliberately kept low by the system provider, in return for which the agency passed the costs of more restricted choice on to its consumers'. Customers would continue to believe that they received an impartial service from their travel agent, and even if they did not it would be exceedingly difficult for them to establish what other options had been available to them at the time their flights were booked. Given the geographical concentration of CRSs, turning to the services of another agent in the locality would be unlikely to prove of any benefit in this regard. For example, in Denver Apollo is the dominant CRS accounting for some two-thirds of travel agency revenues.[20]

The impact of the CRS on the airline industry's structure would not have been so great had more carriers developed their own systems. In reality though, the market has been dominated throughout by just two companies, American and United, as table 2.10 shows. Despite a declining share of agency locations these two carriers until recently have accounted for over 70% of the revenues generated by agency CRSs, by virtue of the fact that they had targeted the larger firms long before the other players in the field had woken up to the fact that a very different game was now being played. For example, in 1985 American and United were able to generate 31% and 17% more revenue respectively than their share of agency locations.[21] Table 2.11 shows the share of agency generated revenue for all CRS's in 1985. Only a part of this additional revenue however can be attributed to the control exerted by CRS owners on travel agents over the supply of such equipment; significant portions have also resulted from the explicit biassing of information displayed on VDU screens and from the use of incentive based commissions, as is made clear below.

By 1986 the five remaining CRSs were accounting for 88% of all airline ticket sales in the US.[22] Locating an airline's CRS equipment in agencies that have had the potential to generate the most bookings has invariably meant concentrating them in the geographical areas surrounding each of the carrier's hubs.[23] As the number of hubs operated by each of the major carriers has increased, so there have been attempts to persuade agents to switch allegiances. In some cases considerable

31

inducements have been provided, for example Feldman (1987) reports a case cited by Northwest at a 1985 congressional hearing, in which United is purported to have offered an agent $500,000 in cash, 10% additional commission on each ticket sale and five years free use of Apollo including all telephone charges, if it would replace Sabre with its own system. This, by no means an isolated case, provides an indication as to just how much additional revenue United anticipated generating from this newly captured agent. A recent estimate by Hirst (1989) suggests that some 75% of US agencies measured in terms of the total amount of revenue they generate are tied in this way.

Table 2.10 **CRS Shares of Agency Locations**

System	1983		1985		1986	
	Number	%	Number	%	Number	%
Sabre	5692	41	8906	35	12200	36
Apollo	3865	28	6263	24	8500	25
Pars	2159	16	3419	13	4250	12
SystemOne	1074	8	4303	17	5300	16
Datas	688	5	2685	10	3800	11
Others	344	2	237	1		
Total	13822		25813		34050	

Sources: Wardell, D. (1987), 'Airline Reservation Systems in the USA', Travel & Tourism Analyst, January, p. 51; Feldman, J. (1987), 'CRS in the USA', Travel & Tourism Analyst, September, p. 7; & 'Note on Airline Reservation Systems' (1984), Harvard Business School, pp. 8-14.

Table 2.11 **CRS Market Shares in 1985**

System	Vendor(s)	% of Locations	% of Agency Generated Revenue
Sabre	American	35	46
Apollo	United	24	28
Pars	TWA/Northwest	13	10
SystemOne	Texas Air	17	10
Datas II	Delta	10	5

Source: Airline Business, January 1988, p. 27.

Having tied in a significant proportion of 'local' agencies there has been little to prevent CRS vendors fully exploiting this situation, other than what usually is referred to as 'political expediency'. Although the more blatant display bias of flight and seat availability practised by CRS owners in the early 1980s was outlawed by the CAB in 1984, a number of relatively more sophisticated attempts at the same have followed.[24] CRS owning airlines have been able to present their flight schedules in a beneficial way by adopting algorithms that have given precedence to their flights. Careful manipulation of departure times and flight duration and the use of weighting techniques to distinguish different types of connections, all aimed at disadvantaging the offerings of rivals, have enabled carriers to continue this post-deregulation tradition. In addition to restricting information about the services offered by competitors, CRS generated market intelligence has enabled marketing managers to achieve a high degree of precision in the targeting of their price discrimination activities, resulting in significantly less revenue dilution than ordinarily would be anticipated.

The ability to control ticket sales using, initially at least, relatively simple techniques to bias information relating to flight availability stems partly from the fact that agents have been in the habit of booking 50% of their sales from information displayed on the first line of the first screen showing.[25] From the CRS parent airline's point of view it would have made little sense to have provided travel agents with a system that would attract travellers away from directly booking with them unless they had some means at their disposal to control the activities of such intermediaries. In addition to the impact of inequities in the display of information on CRSs, the various forms of incentive provided by carriers to induce travel agents to give preference to their services has fundamentally altered the relationship that had previously existed between these two parties. Levine (1987) explored this principal/agent involvement and concluded that the incentive packages devised by airlines had been fashioned on the use of non-linear reward structures in order to automatically favour the use of a single carrier's services. All large airlines irrespective of their CRS owning status, have naturally benefited from this practice as their greater networks have more to attract passengers. As Levine remarked ...'The system rewarded airlines that were particularly adept at paying high incentive commissions for business that was truly incremental...'. CRS ownership has considerably enhanced an airline's ability to control such expenditure. Careful monitoring of individual markets using information produced by a CRS not only reduces unnecessary commission expenses, but also enables an airline to target its marketing efforts in a similarly efficient manner.

As the more overt forms of bias in information display have been made illegal, so the two leading protagonists developed other more sophisticated ways of

33

maintaining a tight control over their markets. Indeed these have been so successful that Wardell (1987) asserts that...'With the opportunity to affect agency carrier selection in so many powerful ways, and with computer services overall profitable ventures in their own right, improper display tactics make little sense for a sophisticated vendor'. That such vendors have been able to exercise considerable control over not only the actions of travel agents and customers, but also of non-CRS owning airlines, stems from the vast amount of market intelligence readily available to them. The latter mentioned have had little choice but to assign their seat reservation functions to one of the five CRS vendors. Besides the financial return that this has provided, the accruing of sensitive information concerning the demand for rivals' products has conveyed with it a considerable degree of market power. For example, the risks that a non-CRS owning airline embarking on a new pricing strategy would incur would be substantial in comparison with those of a CRS vendor undertaking a similar exercise. Whilst the former would face not only the usual uncertainties associated with changing prices, the ability of a CRS owner to negate and indeed turn to its advantage any such amendments would commit such an airline to, metaphorically, 'whistling in the dark'. By contrast American or United undertaking this type of exercise would have had a comparatively clear picture of likely retaliatory action and have adopted tactics in advance aimed at minimising any possible adverse impact, long before initiating the change. Even in the unlikely event of something unforeseen occurring, the ability to respond quickly and with considerable accuracy virtually ensures a safe implementation.

Levine (1987) in an extensive article dealing with airline deregulation highlights some of the more important benefits that a CRS vendor gains from having formed exclusive relationships with travel agents. He comments that...'Through the CRS an airline can track the effect of price changes, see roughly how much of a rival's seat inventory is assigned to a given discount fare classification, measure how much full-fare business it attracts compared to rivals, and track changes in shares of city-pair traffic flows and of market demand sub-segments'. By using this information it can..'..distort market signals to its rivals, leading them to make incorrect decisions'. The phenomenal power that this has conveyed is such as to have ensured the non-contestability of many city-pair markets.

Various estimates have been produced as to how significant an advantage this has proved. For example, Feldman (1987) reports American's chairman as having stated that his airline gained an additional 8-12% in revenue from Sabre equipped agents over that which could ordinarily be expected from equivalent agencies equipped with another company's CRS. A more recent valuation referred to by Hirst (1989) shows that in 1988 Apollo equipped agents produced $44mn each month for United over and above that which could have been expected to be generated by neutral agents in the same markets. He expressed the view that... 'Assuming similar numbers for American, these sums annualised approximate the $981 million which the entire industry earned in profit in 1988'. The Dept of Transportation revealed in a regression analysis conducted in 1988 that relative to the number of seat-kilometres produced the five CRSs generated incremental bookings for their owners ranging from 40% in the case of American to 12% for Texas Air.[26]

The negative impact on the profitability of individual non-CRS owning airlines resulting from this generation of incremental revenue by CRS vendors has been considerable. Table 2.12 reproduces Feldman's (1988) estimate of the impact on the pre-tax profitability of six non-CRS owning carriers caused by a 1% reduction in their average load factors. The information used by this writer was presented by these airlines during a lawsuit taken against American and United. Traffic diversions had had the effect of raising the profitability of the Sabre and Apollo systems by 66% in 1984. The corollary of this was that other carriers had been forced to operate at reduced load factors, resulting in a substantial decrease in their profit margins. Feldman (1988) estimates this reduction in profitability to have been of the order of 38% in 1985 for the airlines cited in the table. The exaggerated impact on profits has given CRS vendors considerable leeway in terms of the financial inducements that they are able to offer travel agents. Once the latter are hooked, the tactics adopted by the vendor take on a more subtle approach, but are none the less efficacious. The manipulation and exploitation of these agents and the commercial relationships they have with their clients has been perfected to a near art form, using the exceptionally clear picture of city-pair markets provided by the increasingly sophisticated CRSs.

With the increasing sophistication of the CRS and the globalisation of airline markets, development costs have burgeoned. Whilst by 1990 the profitability of the two largest systems, Sabre and Apollo, remained in the 20% category, the smaller companies were not faring nearly so well. In many respects the relative advantage of exclusively owning a CRS had been reduced, partly as a result of the high level of merger activity between 1986 and 1988. Responding to this change, CRS-owning airlines have sought to share the development cost burden by either merging their CRS subsidiary with another carrier's CRS or selling off part of their system. After an abortive attempt to merge its Datas II system with Sabre in 1989, Delta agreed to create Worldspan jointly with Northwest and TWA, the owners of Pars, reducing the number of systems in the US market to four. In 1990 Continental Airline Holdings, owners of System One, sold 50% of their CRS to Electronic Data Systems, a subsidiary of General Motors. More recently an attempt to merge Sabre and Covia failed to gain approval from the US Administration. A merger of the Worldspan and System One CRSs also has been raised as being a distinct possibility.

**Table 2.12   Impact of a 1% Reduction in Load Factor
per Domestic Departure on Six Carriers in 1985**

	Actual	Adjusted	% Decrease
Average passengers enplaned per domestic aircraft departure (%)	58.0	57.0	1.7
Total enplanements ('000)	70,608	69,373	1.7
Revenue passenger miles (mn)	45,934	45,127	1.7
Average seat miles (mn)	79,470	79,470	
Load factor (%)	57.8	56.8	1.7
Total revenue ($mn)	6,928	6,818	1.6
Operating expense plus interest	6,702	6,680	0.3
Pre-tax profit ($mn)	226	138	38.9
Profit margin (%)	3.3	2.0	38.0

Source: Feldman, J. (1988), 'CRS and Fair Airline Competition', Travel & Tourism Analyst, p. 20.

Links between US and European CRSs have been under development for several years, but the first major step towards establishing a genuinely global CRS was announced in March 1992 with the formation of Galileo International, a merger of the Apollo and Galileo systems. Alliances have also developed with Australasian, Canadian and Far Eastern CRSs, as table 2.13, which provides a summary of the current position in the world CRS market, indicates. With Galileo International now in existence, it would seem likely that the industry now will rapidly consolidate into three global systems.

Table 2.13   Increasing CRS Market Concentration

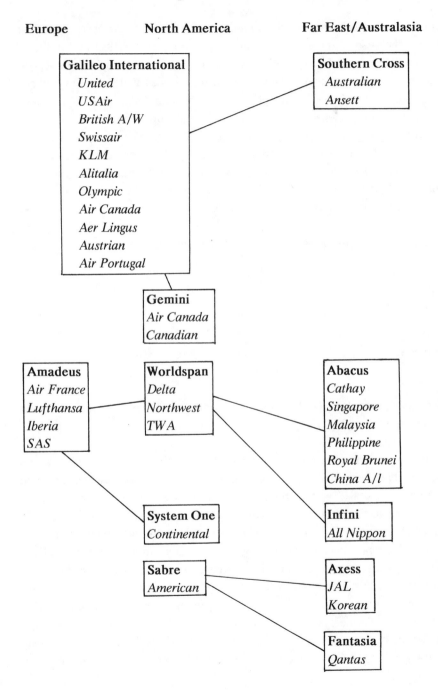

Europe   North America   Far East/Australasia

Galileo International
United
USAir
British A/W
Swissair
KLM
Alitalia
Olympic
Air Canada
Aer Lingus
Austrian
Air Portugal

Southern Cross
Australian
Ansett

Gemini
Air Canada
Canadian

Amadeus
Air France
Lufthansa
Iberia
SAS

Worldspan
Delta
Northwest
TWA

Abacus
Cathay
Singapore
Malaysia
Philippine
Royal Brunei
China A/l

System One
Continental

Infini
All Nippon

Sabre
American

Axess
JAL
Korean

Fantasia
Qantas

2.3 The Impact of Frequent Flyer Programs

A major attempt to influence customer choice has involved the use of frequent flyer programs. The first of these was introduced by American in 1982 and provided travellers with a reward for continuing to make use of the company's services. This attempt to increase consumer loyalty is based on the idea that the more flights a passenger takes with the airline the greater their reward. Although there has been nothing preventing passengers from participating in more than one program, the award levels are constructed so as to encourage exclusivity of use.[27] For example, a frequent flyer scheme recently operated by United provides one domestic upgrade for 10,000 miles flown with the company, whilst for 40,000 miles a return trip to Europe is offered.[28] Table 2.14 gives details of the number of members each major carrier's scheme has attracted.

Table 2.14	Frequent Flyer Program Membership
American	14.2m
United	13.3m
Delta	10.1m
Continental	9.1m
Northwest	8.6m
USAir	7.8m

Source: Humphreys, B.K. (1991), 'Are FFPs anticompetitive?', Avmark Aviation Economist, July/August, p. 12.

The primary aim has been to attract passengers travelling frequently on business who, given that their companies are footing the bill, usually have no personal incentive to economise on air travel. A strong vested interest exists for such customers both to trade up and to undertake more journeys than would be strictly warrented. As a consequence, such travellers are highly important to airlines as they generate a disproportionately large amount of revenue. In 1990, for example, if frequent flyers are defined as individuals taking more than twelve airline trips annually, then approximately 3% of US passengers accounted for 27% of all trips and 40% of airline revenues.[29] In essence, a common area of potential conflict between individual employees and their employers has been exploited by airlines. By pandering to the egos of business travellers, carriers have been extremely successful in adding business class travel to the list of perceived status symbols. Only the recent worldwide recession has altered the balance back in favour of the cost conscious company and its shareholders.

Network size has been a particularly important factor for travellers in their choice as to which scheme to participate in. Not surprisingly the larger carriers have been the main beneficiaries, as the choice of leisure destinations they are able to offer is invariably much greater than those offered by the smaller operators. Code-sharing alliances with regional airlines have extended this choice and so strengthened brand loyalty. An important additional influencing factor here has been the added precision of the CRS, which has enabled their owners to perfect their incentive packages in such a way as to minimise the rewards paid to committed travellers, so reducing wastage. Other less well-endowed carriers with smaller networks and not owning a CRS have had little option but to follow suit and establish their own programs. Attempting to reduce their relative competitive disadvantage in this way merely has had the effect of raising the cost of holding on to their existing customers, without it generating the additional revenue to offset the cost.

2.4 The Impact of Code-Sharing Alliances

Prior to 1984 there had been very few code-sharing alliances formed between the large carriers and commuter airlines.[30] Over the next two years however, a considerable transformation occurred, so that by the middle of 1986 all of the twelve major carriers and four of the national airlines had entered into code-sharing alliances with operators of commuter services.[31] Indeed, nearly all of the largest fifty commuter carriers had formed code-sharing alliances with a major airline by 1985, companies participating in these agreements accounting for over 75% of the passengers carried by the whole of the commuter airline industry.[32] Table 2.15 lists the agreements in force between the major airlines and the largest 30 commuter carriers in 1986.

Table 2.15   **Code-Sharing Alliances in 1986**

Regional Carrier	Enplaned Passengers('000)	Major Partner(s)
Air Wisconsin	2026.0	United
Metro	1494.0	American/Eastern
Mid-Pacific	1286.9	Continental
Atlantic Southeast	1156.0	Delta
Henson	1152.0	Piedmont
Horizon Air	1147.8	Alaska

39

Regional Carrier	Enplaned Passengers('000)	Major Partner(s)
Simmons	1092.5	American/Northwest
Britt	985.0	Continental/Eastern
Air Midwest	923.0	American/East'n/TWA
PBA	856.9	Continental
Skywest	763.0	Delta
Express Airlines I	754.0	Northwest
Aspen	640.0	United
Comair	634.8	Delta
Pan Am Express	555.1	Pan Am
West Air	544.9	United
Pennsylvania A/l	534.3	USAir
Business Express	525.0	Delta
Bar Harbor	453.0	Eastern
Brockway	429.2	Piedmont
Wings West	408.5	American
Suburban	406.3	USAir
Royale	385.4	Continental
CCAir	380.2	Piedmont
Rocky Mountain	362.2	Continental
Chautauqua	358.1	USAir
Gull Air	354.0	Continental
Command	322.2	American
Metro Express II	295.0	American
Crown Airways	288.3	USAir

Source: Feldman, J. (1987), 'Regional Airlines in the USA', Travel & Tourism Analyst, May, p. 22.

This phenomenon had come about as a direct result of the continuing development of the hub and spoke systems adopted by the major airlines. The economies of scope that are possible to achieve with this type of route configuration are exploited fully only when all possible locations are being served. As a consequence, the rapid development of nationwide route networks had become a key priority by the mid 1980s. In order to operate profitably in low density markets it was essential to make use of small turbo-prop aircraft, typically seating up to 30 passengers. Large carriers had neither experience of these markets nor did they possess this type of equipment. Following the development of traffic hubs by the major airlines, commuter carriers became increasingly dependent on these companies for their traffic. This growing interdependence invariably worked against the interests of the smaller companies. For example, Oster and Pickrell (1986) put forward the view that commuter airlines...'..might be pitted against one another in the major carrier's battle for control of a hub and encouraged by the major carrier partner to provide economically high levels of service in a fight for market share'.

The benefits of code-sharing to a large CRS owning carrier were considerable. The ability to attract additional clients through the manipulation of travel agents, in part aided by the use of frequent flyer programs, was considerably enhanced as route networks became more extensive.[33] Although the code-sharing services operated by commuter carriers in conjunction with, and on behalf of, their partners were still nominally considered to be independent flights, to all intents and purposes they formed an integral part of the larger carriers' route networks. In effect the commuter companies had had little option but to form such alliances in order to survive. In the process they lost their autonomy and became increasingly integrated with the major airlines.[34] This dependency of virtually all of the smaller independent carriers proved to be highly effective in removing an important source of potential rivalry.

2.5 Summary

The various factors outlined above have acted in a synergetic way to provide large airlines with an even greater competitive advantage over their smaller and less well endowed rivals. The imaginative and mostly unconstrained exploitation of the CRS though has been a critical factor in enabling their owners to gain the full advantage of their reconfigured route systems. Table 2.16 summarises in chart form the consolidation that has occurred in the US airline industry since 1978. The survivors of the restructuring process are listed in table 2.17, together with their most recent respective market shares. (In table 2.16 Major carriers are shown in normal type and National airlines in italics.) The cumulative effect of the various features of the deregulated airline industry discussed above is analysed in the following chapter.

Table 2.16   Restructuring of the US Airline Industry

Carrier   1979 1980 1981 1982 1983 1984 1985 1986 1987 1988 1989 1990 1991

American---American
Air California--/↗
                              America West----------------------------America West
Continental---Continental
Texas Int'nal------------------/↗   ↗
Eastern--↗---------------------------
Frontier--\   ↗
                    People Express----↘--------------
Delta---↗-------------------Delta
Western--↗
Northwest--Northwest
Hughes Airwest---*Republic*------------------------------------/↗
North Central-------/↗
Southern-----------↗
National-----------
Pan Am---------------\↘--Pan Am
Southwest---Southwest
TWA--↗----------------------TWA
Ozark---/↗
United---United
Air Wisconsin---
USAir---USAir
Pacific Southwest---↗   ↗
Piedmont---/↗
Braniff--------------------------   ----------------------------------
Alaska---Alaska
              Jet America------------------/↗
                    Horizon--Horizon
Aloha--Aloha
Hawaiian--Hawaiian
Alaska Int. Air-----------------------*Markair*------------------------------------Markair
Midway--Midway
                    Midwest Express----------------*Midwest Express*
                              Trump Shuttle------*Trump Shuttle*
WestAir--WestAir

Table 2.17   **The 1993 Survivors of Deregulation**

Major Airlines	% Market Share (RPKs) (Jan-Sept 1993)
American	20.8
America West	2.3
Continental	8.6
Delta	17.3
Northwest	12.5
Southwest	3.5
TWA	4.8
United	21.3
USAir	7.3
National Carriers	
Air Wisconsin	<0.1
Alaska	0.7
Aloha	<0.1
Atlantic S.E.	<0.1
Hawaiian	0.4
Horizon	<0.1
Markair	0.1
Midwest Express	0.1
USAir Shuttle	<0.1

Source: Air Transport World, February 1994, pp. 118 - 120.

Notes

1. Richard Caves (1962) argued that as a result of CAB policy rivalry could be expected to occur through variations in service quality. Air Transport and Its Regulators: An Industry Study, Harvard University Press.
2. In 1942 the CAB approved an agreement which committed participants to honouring each others tickets for the carriage of passengers and their luggage. 'Interline Traffic Agreement - Passengers', Air Traffic Resolution 5.65.
3. Interlining involves a passenger transferring from one carrier to another at an intermediate point in the course of his or her journey. In 1977 interlining domestic traffic constituted 24.6% of total city-pair RPM's. By 1984 this figure

had fallen to 10%. (Phillips, L. T. (1987), 'Air Carrier Activity at Major Hub Airports and Changing Interline Practices in the United States' Airline Industry', Transportation Research A, Vol. 21A, No. 3, p. 218.)

4. So called 'grandfather' rights relate to the use of take-off and landing slots by incumbent airlines at congested airports. The allocation of these scarce resources is usually determined by individual airport committees, which mostly consist of airline employees. Historical precedence forms the main criterion in this apportioning process.

5. In 1987/8 American acquired two bankrupt commuter carriers which had been providing feeder services on its behalf. AMR Eagle Inc. was formed in mid 1987 to operate services previously provided by Air Midwest, American's code-sharing partner based at Nashville. In January 1988 AVAir, the American Eagle operator at Raleigh/Durham, filed a Chapter 11 bankruptcy petition and the acquisition process was repeated. A further three feeder service partners were acquired in 1988, but not as a result of commercial failure. These carriers were Wings West (Los Angeles/San Francisco), Command Airways (New York) and Simmons Airlines (Chicago). Details of these acquisitions are contained in Commuter World, 'The Integration of American's Eagles', November 1988, pp. 24-28; and 'Under the Eagle's Wing', January 1989, pp. 28-32.

6. 'Carriers who had previously been considered Supplementals, such as World, began making the New York-Los Angeles route the most price competitive in the world.' Gialloreto, L. (1988), Strategic Airline Management: The Global War Begins, Pitman, p. 28.

7. '...by 1982 none of the airlines flying the transcontinental routes was making as much as a 1% return on sales.' Gialloreto, L. (1988), supra note 7, p. 28.

8. Caves, D. W., Christensen, L. R., & Tretheway, M. W. (1984), 'Economies of Density versus economies of scale: why trunk and local service airlines costs differ', Rand Journal of Economics, Vol. 15, No. 4, pp. 471-89.

9. Gloria Hurdle, speaking for the US Dept. of Justice, developed this point in connection with Northwest Orient's proposed acquisition of Republic. Comments in the NWA-Republic Acquisition Case (Docket 43754), Dept. of Justice, Washington, DC, 1986.

10. The relationship between the maximum possible number of connections and the number of spokes radiating from a traffic hub is given by the formula:

$$C = \frac{n(n-1)}{2}$$

where C refers to the number of connections and n to the number of spokes. Table 2.18 explores the effect on C as n is increased.

Table 2.18   Characteristics of Hub and Spoke Networks

No. of Spokes	Maximum No. of Connections	Connectivity Ratio
5	15	3.0:1
10	55	5.5:1
20	210	10.5:1
30	465	15.5:1
40	820	20.5:1
50	1275	25.5:1
100	5050	50.5:1
200	20100	100.5:1

$$[\text{Connectivity Ratio} = \frac{\underline{n} + 0.5}{2}]$$

Source: Doganis, R. & Dennis, N. (1989), 'Lessons in Hubbing', Airline Business, March, p. 42.

11. USAir, known as Allegheny Airlines until October 1979, continues to operate its own commuter feeder services under the name Allegheny Commuter.

12. Cost per ATK for local service carriers was higher than that of trunk airlines, but in the main was more than accounted for by the considerably shorter average sector length of the former.

13. 'The key to success is the exclusivity of the routes rather than the structure of the network.' Toh, R. S. & Higgins, R. G. (1985), 'The Impact of Hub and Spoke Network Centralization and Route Monopoly on Domestic Airline Profitability', Transportation Journal, Summer, p. 27.

14. USAir's route system reveals the carrier's concentration on small and medium sized locations.

15. USAir - Piedmont Acquisition Case, Docket 44719, US Dept of Transportation, Office of Hearings, Washington, DC, September 1987, pp. 32-50 and appendices C, D and E.

16. Southwest, for example, has served a number of specialist niche markets particularly in connection with its operations from the downtown airports at Dallas and Houston.

17. Note on Airline Reservation Systems (1984), Harvard Business School, p. 3.

18. Wardell, D. (1987), 'Airline Reservation Systems in the USA', Travel & Tourism Analyst, January, p. 47.

19. The large increase in the number of agencies equipped with a CRS is partly explained by the advent of inexpensive micro computers.

20. Feldman,J. (1987), 'CRS in the USA', Travel & Tourism Analyst, September, p. 10.
21. Feldman, J. (1988), 'CRS and Fair Airline Competition', Travel & Tourism Analyst, p. 7; and Airline Business (1988), January, p. 27.
22. Feldman, J. (1987), supra note 21, p. 3.
23. Levine, M. E. (1987), 'Airline Competition in Deregulated Markets: Theory, Firm Strategy, and Public Policy', Yale Journal on Regulation, Vol. 4, p. 464.
24. Hirst, R. B. (1989), 'The CRS Mess, 1984-89: From Display Bias to Travel Agency Franchises', American Bar Association, Forum on Air and Space Law, Seattle, May, pp. 1-3.
25. Wardell, D. (1987), supra note 19, p. 48, estimates that between 70% and 90% of bookings have been made on the basis of information displayed on the first screen showing.
26. Hirst, R. B., supra note 25, p. 3.
27. Passengers participating in frequent flyer programs belonged to 2.26 such schemes on average in 1989. 'A Multiple Discriminant Approach to Identifying Frequent Flyers in Airline Travel: Some Implications for Market Segmentation, Travel Marketing and Product Differentiation', Toh R. S. & Hu M. Y. (1990), The Logistics & Transportation Review, June, pp.179-97.
28. Executive Flight Planner, ABC International, February 1989.
29. Humphreys, B.K. (1991), 'Are Frequent Flyer Programmes anticompetitive?', Avmark Aviation Economist, July/August, pp. 12-15.
30. Feldman, J. (1987), 'Regional Airlines in the USA', Travel & Tourism Analyst, May, p. 19.
31. The CAB in 1981 had begun classifying airlines on the basis of annual revenues, categorising 'major' carriers as those generating in excess of $1 billion and 'national' carriers as earning between $100 million and $1 billion.
32. Oster, C. V. & Pickrell, D. H. (1986), 'Marketing Alliances and Competitive Strategy in the Airline Industry', Logistics and Transportation Review, Vol. 22, No. 4, p. 372.
33. Feldman, J. (1987), supra note 21, p. 23.
34. Some examples of this are contained in 'Code-sharing: the brass ring can sometimes turn to lead', Air Transport World, June 1988, pp. 190-3; and 'Turmoil and trauma for the code-sharers', Avmark Aviation Economist, March/April 1988, pp. 12-15.

Bibliography

Feldman, J. (1987), 'CRS in the USA', Travel & Tourism Analyst, September, pp. 3-4

Hirst, R. B. (1989), 'The CRS Mess, 1984-89: From Display Bias to Travel Agency Franchises', American Bar Association, Forum on Air and Space Law, Seattle, May, p. 5.

Kanafani, A. (1981), 'Aircraft Technology and Network Structure in Short-Haul Air Transportation', Transportation Research, Vol. 15A, pp. 305-314.

Levine, M. E. (1987), 'Airline Competition in Deregulated Markets: Theory, Firm Strategy, and Public Policy', Yale Journal on Regulation, Vol. 4, pp. 434-36.

Oster, C. V. & Pickrell, D. H. (1986), 'Marketing Alliances and Competitive Strategy in the Airline Industry', Logistics and Transportation Review, Vol. 22, No. 4, p. 383.

Phillips, L. T. (1987), 'Air Carrier Activity at Major Hub Airports and Changing Interline Practices in the United States' Airline Industry', Transportation Research A, Vol. 21A, No. 3.

Toh, R. S. & Higgins, R. G. (1985), 'The Impact of Hub and Spoke Network Centralization and Route Monopoly on Domestic Airline Profitability', Transportation Journal, Summer, pp.16-27.

Wardell, D. (1987), 'Airline Reservation Systems in the USA', Travel & Tourism Analyst, January, p. 52.

3 Explaining the surprise

Within three years of the passing of the 1978 Airline Deregulation Act nearly all US carriers were experiencing a substantial change in their financial performance. A position of high profit making was transformed rapidly into one of heavy losses. (Figure 3.1 traces the financial plight of US carriers over the past fourteen years.) At this stage few observers were willing to apportion much of the blame for this on deregulation. Indeed, it would have been unrealistic to have done so as economic recession and the protracted strike by air traffic controllers in the early 1980s were also major contributory factors. Nonetheless, the freedom for any carrier to enter any interstate city-pair market had made the larger incumbents particularly vulnerable to the lower operating costs and greater flexibility of their new rivals. The former trunk carriers were faced with a stark choice they had either to instigate policies that rapidly would improve their relative positions vis a vis new entrants to the interstate markets or face extinction.[1]

After an initial honeymoon period the realisation that not all could benefit from deregulation became apparent. The early responses of trunk carriers to this alarming prospect were comparatively crude, often giving rise to the appearance of panic. In many respects it was a time for experimentation. Previous managerial experience gained in the industry provided little or no insight as to how to best tackle the problem. Certain of the tactics adopted proved disastrous for their companies, as was the case for Braniff. Lessons were rapidly learned however and in varying measure successful strategies developed. A greater insight into the restructuring process triggered by deregulation developed. By the mid 1980s it had become clear that without government intervention the industry would eventually evolve to exhibit a high degree of market concentration.

Figure 3.1   **Financial Results of US Carriers**
(Net Profit on all Scheduled Operations)

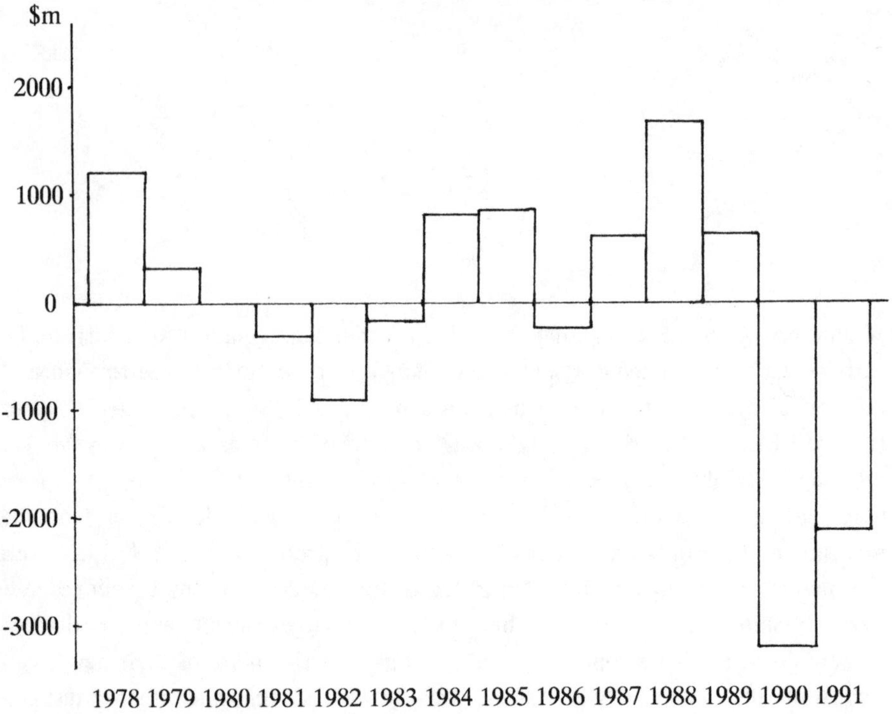

3.1 Reducing Competitive Disadvantage

The early route expansion strategies developed by a number of the former trunk carriers were rapidly shown to be unsuccessful, as the high density markets that had been the focus of this expansion also became the target of other airlines. One such group were the former charter operators, which at the resulting low fares were able to operate profitably in these markets. By contrast, the high operating costs of the large incumbents rendered their operations unprofitable. The fleets of wide-bodied aircraft operated by these airlines became a considerable disadvantage as hub and spoke route networks began to be developed.[2] The smaller aircraft operated by the former local service carriers coupled with their more centralised regional networks provided them with both flexibility and an efficient supply of feeder traffic. That they were therefore better placed during this route expansion phase is clear. An additional factor here being that many of their markets generated insufficient traffic levels to prove attractive to potential competitors, so enabling carriers like USAir to continue to maintain a monopolistic position on many of their routes.

Table 3.1 summarises the options facing incumbent carriers in their response to competition; whilst table 3.2 identifies three distinct stages in the development of former trunk carrier strategy following deregulation.

Table 3.1   Strategic Response Options to Increased Competition

Defensive Tactics - Operating Within the New Commercial Environment

Cost Reducing Activities:

Labour	- implement a two tier wage structure
	- improve productivity
	- reduce demarcation
	- reorganise management
	- deunionise
	- declare bankruptcy to force labour changes
Aircraft	- purchase/lease more efficient aircraft
	- downsize
Network	- operate a hub and spoke route system

Revenue Generating Activities:

- develop a CRS
- introduce a frequent flyer program
- vary travel agency commission levels
- increase service frequency
- enter into code-sharing alliances
- improve in-flight service
- increase advertising
- price discriminate

Offensive Tactics - Transforming the New Competitive Environment

Building Entry Barriers:

- control CRS information supplied to travel agents (biassing display & contractual arrangements)
- control airport gates & runway slots
- tie in commuter airlines

Given the lower operating costs of new entrant and former charter only airlines, an obvious early response of incumbents involved them in attempts to reduce their operating costs. Not surprisingly, the major burden of these cost cutting exercises involved company employees. The most spectacular instance of this being the approach adopted by Continental, which invoked bankruptcy proceedings in order to replace its relatively expensive unionised workforce. This had the effect of reducing at a stroke its unit labour cost by some 36%.[3] A less drastic means of reducing these costs, adopted by a number of carriers, involved the adoption of a two tier wage structure. The advantage of this was that it avoided antagonising existing employees, whilst at the same time allowing companies the freedom to recruit new staff at significantly lower levels of remuneration. That airlines felt compelled to reduce wage costs was clearly evident when comparisons were made between incumbents and new entrants. For example, in 1984 the cost per employee incurred by People Express was of the order of one third of that borne by USAir.[4] One reason for the lower operating costs of the new entrants stemmed from their ability to obtain significantly more output from their employees. Flight crews, for example, worked much longer hours per month than their former trunk counterparts. Demarcation of tasks was also reduced to a minimum by new entrants, further enhancing their higher labour productivity.

Table 3.2　　　　　　　　**Evolving Commercial Strategy**

Stage I　　　　　　　　　**Euphoria**

Airline Type	*Strategy Adopted*	*Main Impact*
Trunk	High density routes targeted	Intense price competition
	Low density routes abandoned	Reduced feeder traffic
Local Service	Interstate routes targeted	Reduced revenue loss to other carriers
New Entrant	Entry to high density routes with emphasis on low fares	Intense price competition

Stage II　　　　　　　　　**Protectionism**

Airline Type	*Strategy Adopted*	*Main Impact*
Trunk	Hub & Spoke development	Economies of density & scope
	Labour cost reductions	Lower unit cost
	Raising productivity	Lower unit cost
	Biassing CRS display	Greater revenue generation

| Local Service | Alliances/Mergers with Trunk carriers | Ensure feed & aid marketing |

Stage III	**Stage Management**	
Airline Type	*Strategy Adopted*	*Main Impact*
Major	Exploitation of CRS	Greater revenue generation
	Acquisition of Commuter Feeders	Greater cost & revenue control
	Acquisition of National Carriers/Mergers	Exploiting full economies of scope
		Elimination of rivals

A second means by which trunk carriers attempted to reduce their operating costs involved them reorienting their route networks into hub and spoke systems. As is made clear in the preceding chapter, this enabled the larger airlines to exploit the substantial economies of scope and density inherent in such systems. At the same time concentrating services at particular locations made it difficult for other carriers to gain access to runway slots and terminal gates at these cities during peak traffic times[5], so enabling the former trunk carriers to capture more of the full fare business market. This had the effect of raising their average yields whilst simultaneously increasing the cost per full fare equivalent passenger carried for their rivals.[6] Additionally, by operating a higher frequency of services from traffic hubs than their competitors, airlines were able to gain higher proportions of the total traffic as a result of the familiar S curve relationship.[7] A summary of the various sources of competitive advantage by carrier type apparent during the first few years following deregulation is given in table 3.3.

Table 3.3   Sources of Competitive Advantage by Carrier Type

Feature	New Entrant	Local Service	Charter	Domestic Trunk	International Trunk
Unit Cost	#		#		
Network Size				#	
CRS				#	#
Slots/Gates		#		#	#
Route Monopoly		#		#	
Traffic Hub		#		(#)	
Fleet	#	#			
Quality		#		#	#

Despite these various attempts to improve efficiency, the former trunk airlines continued to operate at a substantial cost disadvantage relative to new entrants to the interstate markets. Given that it was effectively impossible for them to match the cost levels of the newcomers, other that is than by declaring themselves bankrupt and effectively starting again, their only alternative lay in preventing their rivals acquiring high yielding traffic. To a certain degree this had been achieved by the adoption of hub and spoke route systems, which had had the effect of restricting access to new entrants of the traffic originating and terminating at these hubs. The most important breakthrough with regard to this was brought about by the use of CRS's in controlling the flow of information to the new points of sale in the industry, namely retail travel agencies.

3.2 Developing Competitive Advantage

Deregulation brought about a fundamental change in the point of sale of airline seats, with passengers turning to independent travel agencies for what they consider to be impartial advice. The enormous increase in the number of options available to airline users, both in terms of the number of services operated by different carriers and the range of fares on offer, had made it essential for travellers to rely on the services of such agents. By devising a means by which to directly influence the advice these companies were giving to their clients about the options that existed for their intended journeys, the way was open for carriers to divert more traffic to their operations. Whilst direct ownership of such agencies would have provoked an immediate public outcry of unfair competition, CRS vendors had no need to resort such action. Because of the latter's need for direct instantaneous access to information about seat and fare availability and by being in the unique position of being able to supply this, a small number of fortuitous airlines were able to exert a high degree of control over the reservations made by travel agents on behalf of their clients. Of course all carriers have been able to vary their inducements to travel agents in order to directly influence booking activities, but by not being able to provide direct electronic access to reservations data non-CRS owning carriers were at a considerable disadvantage in this regard.[8]

Control over the activities of travel agents was achieved in two ways: firstly by varying the amount of sales commission paid and secondly through the biassing of information displayed on CRS's supplied to such agents. The former has been devised in such a way so as to reward most those agents who have booked large numbers of passengers on the CRS vendor's flights. These higher percentage commissions ordinarily were paid only to companies that achieved designated target levels.[9] A financial incentive was therefore used as a means to influence the agent's choice as to which information to pass on to the customer. To further limit the agent's decision making ability CRS vendors conspired to bias the information they made available.[10] The net effect of these two attempts to influence the activities of travel agents were to transform what on the surface would appear to have been a competitive marketplace for flight information, into one which in reality consisted of a few very carefully orchestrated, geographically delineated monopolies.[11]

Another important means by which airlines sought to enhance their revenue has been through the use of price discrimination. This was an unexpected outcome of deregulation, as policy makers had anticipated that the ensuing competitive environment would make the practice unviable.[12] The peaking demand characteristics of airline markets are such as to allow considerable variation in price, partly due to the inability of carriers - even in competitive markets - to vary supply to the same extent.[13] The key to achieving the full benefits of such a policy rests in an ability to minimise revenue dilution. Ordinarily discriminatory pricing necessitates the existence of monopoly or highly collusive oligopoly, as it is only in these types of market that firms are able to exercise the necessary control over their customers. The non storable nature of the service however alters this situation. The vast amount of information gathered by CRS's has enabled their owners to fine tune their price discrimination activities, allowing them to extract even more economic rent; their non-CRS owning rivals thereby earning less as a consequence. Without the ownership of such equipment, airlines, unless operating in highly specialised niche markets, had little option but to relinquish their seat reservation activities to one of the five (now four) CRS vendors. The resulting dependency has provided the CRS owner with what normally would be regarded as highly confidential data. To then add what seems insult to injury, CRS vendors are able extract a substantial amount of revenue in the form of fees from these carriers.

3.3 Analysing the Net Effect

The business of extracting economic rent through careful manipulation of the fare at which each seat is offered became of supreme importance. The commercial advantage derived in this way has more than offset the higher operating costs of the larger carriers, enabling them to place less reliance on cost reduction measures. Figures 3.2 and 3.3 provide, by way of a theoretical example, an attempt to illustrate this point. The initial operating cost advantage of the new entrant B is clearly shown in figure 3.2. Whilst this differential has been reduced by the established carrier A implementing a cost cutting programme, in relative terms it continues to be disadvantaged. If our hypothetical incumbent airline owns a CRS, its considerably enhanced ability to extract economic rent can result in this disadvantage being overturned, as is demonstrated in figure 3.3. The continued refinement of the large firm's marketing effort, predominantly a product of continuing investment in its CRS, eventually has the effect of reversing the initial positions of our two airlines.

This is demonstrated in the two figures by first converting the total revenue generated by each carrier for the route in question into an equivalent number of full fare passengers. For this it is necessary to select a normal (full) single fare. The total numbers of passengers carried by each airline are represented in the diagrams by way of an overall % load factor. It is assumed that the newcomer has to offer more of its seats at greater rates of discount than its rival, and as a consequence this reduces its full fare equivalent load factor. Initially it derives a competitive advantage from its greater efficiency, but as the incumbent airline begins to implement the various measures discussed above this is slowly whittled away. Eventually the operating cost per ASK of the established airline will be significantly less than that of its 'low cost' rival at their respective revenue adjusted load factors.

Figure 3.2   **Facing A Low Cost Rival**

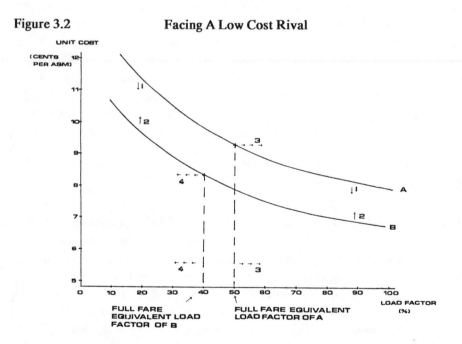

Four effects have conspired to bring this about and these are represented in figure 3.2 by the arrows marked 1 to 4 respectively. The first is the result of the various attempts by the established carrier A to reduce its operating costs. The second stems from the tactics adopted by A to raise the operating costs of B. The third from A's ability to generate more economic rent, whilst the final effect represents the effect of B being forced to offer greater amounts of discount to its passengers in order to maintain load factor. Each of these is now explored in more detail.

Figure 3.3   Developing a Competitive Advantage

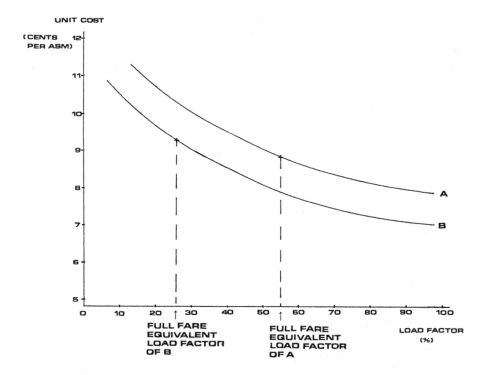

The improvement in operating cost experienced by A has resulted from both a reduction in the basic cost of its input factors and the more efficient use of these resources. The former primarily has entailed the lowering of labour costs and the use of more efficient aircraft. The latter has involved attempts at improving the productivity of both the labour force and aircraft. The adoption of hub and spoke route configurations has enabled airlines to exploit the various economies that are a feature of such systems. Economies of scope have been of particular importance and

57

have enabled the larger carriers to enhance the productive output of both their aircraft and staff. The summation of these various effects is indicated in figure 3.2 by the new unit cost curve shown for A, the scale effects being particularly apparent at the higher load factors.

The raising of a rival's costs also reduces any inherent cost advantage and ultimately may result in its demise. For example, forcing a competitor to undertake an expensive advertising campaign is one classic means by which established firms are able to force up costs.[14] Of particular significance in the airline industry has been the establishment of strategic entry barriers by large carriers at both airports and retail outlets, both of which have raised the operating costs of smaller airlines. These effects are accounted for in the new cost curve for B depicted in figure 3.2.

The third factor relates to the economic rent generating activities of the larger airlines. Obtaining additional rent from customers has been refined to a virtual art form by CRS vendors. The near monopoly conditions created by the clever exploitation of this technology has enabled their owners to increase their price discrimination activities. The vast amount of market information collected and collated has provided this small number of large carriers with the ability to fine tune their operations, thereby further enhancing their revenue generation. Non-CRS owning airlines by comparison are forced to rely on age-old 'guesstimating' techniques. The full fare equivalent load factor for A is increased as a consequence of this additional revenue generation as is indicated in figure 3.2. The fourth and final factor relates to the difficulties of B in its revenue generating activities, the direct result of A's greater ability to attract higher yielding traffic. This is represented in this diagram by a decline in B's full fare load factor.

3.4 Response of the US Administration

The Government's expectation that deregulation would produce a sustainable competitive environment was reinforced by academic arguments concerning the contestability of markets. The theory of contestable markets[15] was developed in the early 1980s and had the effect of focusing attention away from the actual degree of competition existing within a market to a preoccupation with the potential level from firms 'waiting in the wings'. The nub of the theory was that if firms could enter an established market in a costless way (and exit it similarly), then incumbents would be forced to price competitively irrespective of the degree of market concentration.[16] Rather amazingly or so it would now appear, the airline industry was postulated by Bailey and Baumol (1984) amongst others, as presenting..'..a particularly close approximation to contestability'. Evidence from the heavily regulated days of the industry had revealed a general lack of scale economies leading to..'..the almost unanimous conclusion of economists that most airline markets, as well as the airline industry, were not natural monopolies'.[17]

As a result of this research, the clear and unequivocal expectation of most observers of the industry was that..'..the barriers to entry in airline markets..(would)..appear to be quite low, and the number of potential entrants quite high. Thus, there may well be little room for monopoly abuse, even in small airline markets which can support only one carrier at efficient scale.'[18] Thirteen years of deregulation however has resulted in a very different outcome. One that rather unfortunately bears little resemblance to the confidently expressed beliefs of many economists. A number of surprises came with economic freedom as Kahn (1988) has acknowledged. One of the major surprises of deregulation has been the pace at which a few airlines have managed to squeeze out their new rivals and perhaps more importantly the resolute refusal of the Dept. of Transportation to prevent any of the merger and acquisition activity of the mid/late 1980s.[19] A summary of the DoT's approach towards the measurement and analysis of increasing market concentration is contained in Appendix 2.

3.5 Was It All Worth It?

To date it would appear on average that fares are some 15% lower than they could expected to have been if the earlier tight regulatory regime had continued in force.[20] This reduction reflects the real fall in operating costs acheived by most carriers during the 1980s. (Table 3.4 provides details of average yields and unit operating costs for the US domestic airline industry since 1979.) Attempts to trace changes in fare levels are complicated however by the phenomenal amount of price discrimination undertaken by airlines. Although the vast majority of US domestic passengers continue to travel at discounted fare levels as table 3.5 shows, not all passengers have benefited.[21] In certain city-pair markets an increase in real fares has been the outcome, as opponents of deregulation have been able to demonstrate.[22] Protagonists of the policy though have been more than able to counter this criticism by citing examples of city-pair markets in which competition has been, and continues to be, effective in holding down fares and presenting consumers with a considerable element of choice.[23]

Table 3.4   US Domestic Average Yields and Unit Operating Costs

Year	Average Yield (cents/RPM)	Unit Operating Cost (cents/ASM)
1979	9.58	5.99
1980	12.26	7.15
1981	13.75	7.98
1982	12.93	7.78
1983	12.29	7.45
1984	13.19	7.32
1985	12.63	7.51
1986	11.66	6.90
1987	12.08	7.14
1988	12.95	7.52
1989	13.00	
1990	13.25	
1991	13.07	

Source: Statistics for 1979 - 1988 are taken from IATA's Deregulation Watch Fourth Report, 1989. The remaining data relates to major carriers only and is calculated from statistics supplied in the June issues of Air Transport World for 1990, 1991 and 1992.

Table 3.5   Growth of Discounted Fares

Year	Discount Traffic as % of Total	Average Discount (%)
1981	70.6	46.2
1982	77.7	46.2
1983	81.5	48.4
1984	80.7	51.5
1985	85.3	55.9
1986	90.1	61.3
1987	91.3	61.9
1988	91.0	63.2
1989	90.5	66.5

Source: Air Transport World, March 1990, p. 148.

As yet the restructuring of the industry initiated by deregulation is not complete. Further consolidation will increase the already high level of market concentration. Table 3.6 details how domestic market concentration levels have varied over the past sixteen years. With the passage of time it would seem likely that examples of higher real fares being charged by airlines will become more plentiful, as the survivors seek to extract the financial return long denied them. On balance though, given that demand for domestic airline services has more than doubled since 1978, that fares are on average lower in real terms and that standards of safety have improved it would be difficult to conclude that deregulation has been anything other than a success to date. This is not to say that the benefits of deregulation have been universally distributed, nor that there have not been many losers.

Table 3.6   US Carriers Domestic Market Shares 1978-93 (%RPM)

1978		1983		1988		1993[*]	
United	21.1	United	18.7	Texas Air	17.5	American	20.4
American	13.5	American	13.8	United	17.3	United	18.2
Delta	12.0	Delta	11.1	American	17.1	Delta	17.6
Eastern	11.1	Eastern	11.1	Delta	14.1	Northwest	9.7
TWA	9.4	TWA	7.1	USAir	9.5	USAir	9.3
Western	5.0	Republic	4.2	TWA	6.5	Contin'al	9.0
Continental	4.5	Northwest	4.2	Northwest	4.6	Southwest	4.8
Braniff	3.8	Western	3.9	Southwest	2.4	TWA	4.5
National	3.6	Continental	3.5	America West	2.2	Am West	3.2
Northwest	2.6	Pan Am	3.3	Pan Am	2.0	Alaska	1.0
Top 3	46.6		43.6		51.9		56.2
Top 4	57.7		54.7		66.0		65.9
Top 6	72.1		66.0		82.0		84.2
Top 10	86.6		80.9		93.2		97.7

(* First 9 months)

Sources: Air Transport World and Aviation Daily.

3.6 Future Prospects

Attempting to reach an overall impression about the longer term effects of deregulation is by no means an easy task. It is apparent that a very small number of similarly sized and equally endowed megacarriers will ultimately survive the restructuring triggered by deregulation. The demise of Eastern, Midway and Pan Am in 1991 brought this reality a little closer. Nonetheless, the restructuring process still has a little way to go! At present only one major carrier, America West, remains in operation under Chapter 11 bankruptcy protection; Continental and TWA having emerged from this position in 1993. Two other major carriers, Northwest and USAir, have also faced substantial financial difficulties. Only American, Delta and United can be regarded as strong contenders for independent long term survival. Each of these three carriers are now of broadly a similar size and market power, following their more recent acquisitions from bankrupt airlines. In particular, each has been able to expand considerably its international network as a consequence of the dire needs of Eastern, Pan Am and TWA to cover their debts. Whether or not the US Government will view the prospects for competition as acceptable given an airline industry dominated by just four or five megacarriers remains to be seen. The possibility of allowing foreign carriers access to its domestic markets may offer some way out of this dilemma, but appears a large price to pay politically for what may well result in little benefit to consumers given a global alignment of airlines.

To date the ability of the three largest carriers to stage manage their competitive environments has been curtailed as a result of the protection that has been afforded to bankrupt airlines. The desperation of this latter group in their endeavours to generate revenue has produced a number of spectacular price wars, plunging nearly all operators into heavy financial loss during the recent recession. The one exception being Southwest, which has remained consistently profitable. Its low cost - no frills philosophy, to which it has consistently adhered, has proved highly successful in the US domestic market. In the longer term it will be fascinating to observe how and in what manner the surviving megacarriers interact competitively. It remains to be seen how quickly airline managements will adjust to a more stable operating environment, especially one that provides them with fewer opportunities for expansion.

Notes

1. The net aggregate profit of the major and national carriers on domestic operations amounted to some $804 billion in 1978, but by 1982 as a result of deregulation, economic recession and a number of labour disputes this was transformed into a net loss of $1,317 billion. IATA Deregulation Watch - Third Report, 1986, Appendix 2.

2. Kyle, R. & Phillips, L. T.(1985), 'Airline Deregulation: Did Economists Promise Too Much or Too Little', Logistics and Transportation Review, Vol. 21 (1), p. 18.

3. Calculated from statistical data published in Air Transport World and Aviation Daily.

4. Calculated from statistical data published in Air Transport World and Aviation Daily.

5. A survey of gate availability carried out by the Airport Operators Council International in January 1989 is referred to in Airline Business, October 1989, p. 17.

6. This measure is referred to in more detail on page 7.

7. Taneja, N. K. (1968), Flight Transportation Laboratory Report R-68-2, 'Airline Competition Analysis', Massachusetts Institute of Technology.

8. A comparatively recent survey of the commission levels paid to travel agencies during the deregulated era is contained in Airline Business, November 1988, pp. 33-6.

9. Levine, M. E. (1987), 'Airline Competition in Deregulated Markets: Theory, Firm Strategy, and Public Policy', Yale Journal on Regulation, Vol. 4, pp. 454-8.

10. Some early examples of the biassing of information display are contained in 'Note on Airline Reservation Systems', Harvard Business School, 1984, pp. 29-37. More recent evidence of this is contained in Avmark Aviation Economist, May 1987, pp. 19-20; and in Appendix 7 of the European Civil Aviation Conference submission in connection with the US Dept. of Transportation's investigation into the CRS industry, published in 1988.

11. For example, even though in reality there may be six carriers offering a service from A to B at about the time a client wishes to travel, if the agent only indicates one such option as being available, then to all intents and purposes as far as this traveller is concerned this particular market is monopolistic. By controlling the agencies in their main traffic generating locations in this way CRS vendors have been able to confer near monopoly status on a significant number of the city-pair markets in which they operate.

12. Levine, M. E. (1987), supra note 9, pp. 413-4.

13. In most land-based urban public transport systems some two thirds of the available rolling stock is required purely for peak operations. Profitable operation under these conditions is hardly ever accomplished.

14. Salop, S. C. & Scheffman, D. T. (1983), 'Raising Rivals' Costs', American Economic Association Papers and Proceedings, May, pp. 267-71.

15. Baumol, W. J., Panzar, J. C., & Willig, R. D. (1982), Contestable Markets and the Theory of Industry Structure, Harcourt-Brace-Jovanovich.

16. For a market to display perfect contestability requires costless entry and exit and an absence of sunk costs, in effect the complete non-existence of entry barriers.

17. Kyle, R. & Phillips, L.T. (1985), 'Airline Deregulation: Did Economists Promise Too Much or Too Little?', Logistics and Transportation Review, Vol. 21 (1), p. 13.

18. White, L. J. (1979), 'Economies of Scale and the Question of 'Natural Monopoly' in the Airline Industry', Journal of Air Law and Commerce, Vol. 44, p. 548.

19. As witnessed by the approval granted to a number of highly questionable acquisitions and mergers during the period 1985-8. Fisher and Jordan have each examined in some detail this particular aspect of deregulation. (Fisher, F. M. (1987), 'Horizontal Mergers: Triage and Treatment', Economic Perspectives, Vol. 1, No. 2, PP. 23-40. Jordan, W. A. (1988),'Problems Stemming from Airline Mergers and Acquisitions', Transportation Journal, Summer, PP. 9-30.)

20. '.it appears that the figure of 15% savings does represent a reliable estimate of the current effect of deregulation on the overall level of airline fares.' Pickrell, D. (1991), 'The Regulation and Deregulation of US Airlines' in K. Button (ed.), Airline Deregulation - International Experiences, David Fulton Publishers, p. 29.

21. By contrast the Association of European Airlines (AEA) estimated that in 1985 some 57% of intra-European passengers travelled at discounted fares averaging some 38% of normal levels.

22. For example: Shepherd, W. G. (1988), 'Competition, Contestability, and Transport Mergers', International Journal of Transport Economics, Vol. XV, No. 2, pp. 113-28; and Humphreys, B. (1987), 'The Myth of 'Contestability'', Avmark Aviation Economist, January, pp. 7-8.

23. A 1988 study undertaken by the US General Accounting Office concluded that dominant airlines were charging higher fares at a number of concentrated hubs than was the case at other locations. This conclusion was challenged by the US Air Transport Association which had commissioned its own research into the matter. Its main finding was that competition between hubs was increasing,

although it did acknowledge the existence of slightly higher fares at certain hubs. Aviation Week & Space Technology, 12 June 1989, pp. 312-313.

Bibliography

Bailey, E. E. & Baumol, W. J. (1984), 'Deregulation and the Theory of Contestable Markets', Yale Journal on Regulation, Vol. 1:111, p. 128.

Kahn, A. E. (1988), 'Surprises of Airline Deregulation', American Economics Association Papers and Proceedings, May, pp. 316-22.

4 Liberalisation –
The European approach

For the past forty years the economic regulations constraining Western Europe's air transport industry have become progressively less effective. With certain notable exceptions this situation has arisen not as a result of governments freely deciding to interpret existing policies more liberally, but rather as a consequence of pressure from consumers, factions within the industry and more recently, from the European Commission. Retrenchment best describes the overall governmental response to this onslaught. In general, European States have been reluctant to relinquish control of what have been important instruments of public policy. The major distinction between the period up to the mid 1980s and that since is that during the latter governments have had little choice but to formally acknowledge the desirability of liberalising their restrictive policies.

A commonly held view is that the experience the US has gained from deregulating its domestic airline sector provides a good insight as to the likely effects of liberalisation on Western Europe's scheduled industry. Whilst it is undoubtedly true that the lessons assimilated by US carriers as to how best to survive the rigours of a considerably more competitive environment have exerted a strong influence on the strategic behaviour of both airlines and regulators, in many important respects the two situations are very different.

The most basic of these differences relates to the obvious fact that in Europe there are no fewer than 22 autonomous States[1], each with their own language, culture and administrative procedures, whilst the US comprises a single nation with its populous conversing (mostly) in the same tongue. As a result, some 80% of all airline journeys within Europe are international. Average distance travelled is 60% of that in the US, with most flights being of under two hours duration. As a consequence, rail transport, is, and in the future has a greater potential to be, a strong competitor. In addition, the overall intra-European air transport market is considerably smaller than its US domestic equivalent. A further differentiating feature is that non-scheduled services account for over one half of the demand for

67

air travel in Western Europe.[2] Some 90% of this traffic is accounted for by inclusive tour passengers, mostly comprising sunseekers from Northern Europe holidaying in Mediterranean resorts.[3] Within the US this non-scheduled sector has never accounted for more than 5% of total demand.

In many respects deregulation of the US's international airline services provides a closer parallel to the situation prevailing in Western Europe. Whereas the US had a comparatively easy task in fundamentally altering the economic rules governing its domestic airline industry, its experience with negotiating bilateral agreements with individual states has been far from straightforward. The industry's use as an instrument of public policy often rendering the negotiating procedure both complex and time consuming.

Despite moves towards the formation of a federal Europe, as exemplified in the signing of the Single European Act in June 1983 by the Prime Ministers of the Member States of the European Union, each government continues to pursue its own idiosyncratic national interest. The protectionist attitudes adopted by most European Governments in the post war years towards their flag carrying airlines continues, albeit in slightly more subtle guise. As a consequence, full scale economic deregulation of the industry, whether rapidly or gradually achieved, has never been the remotest possibility.

A competitive airline market as free of state imposed economic controls as is compatible with this objective is perhaps the most accurate way of expressing the European Commission's desires. Given the US experience to date it may well be that if left entirely to market forces Europe's airline industry would be supplied most efficiently by just two carriers.[4] The economies of scope and scale inherent in air transport systems are substantial and are exhausted only at very high output levels. Whilst it would be commercially feasible for Europe's scheduled airline sector to rapidly restructure, it would probably be politically unacceptable. It would seem unlikely that the economically stronger Member States of the European Union would be prepared to see their flag carriers acquired by other airlines. Those countries of a lesser status may have little option but to accept this, being a price they have to pay for Community Membership, always assuming that the Commission is willing to sanction such action.

In order for Europe's carriers to be able to compete effectively with both the survivors of US deregulation and powerful low cost Far Eastern based airlines they are going to have to be considerably larger. Given the political unacceptability of major companies disappearing and the Commission's attitude to enhanced market power achieved through merger or acquisition, collusive activities of various kinds would appear to be the only viable option. It seems likely that two, or possibly three, airline consortia may well be the end result of the restructuring process in Europe.

The purpose of this chapter is to examine the ways in which air transport regulatory policy has evolved in Western Europe. The various ways in which the regulations have been circumvented and the responses of scheduled carriers and regulators to the large and evolving charter market are analysed. The various proposals put forward by the Commission are examined in detail and assessed in terms of their impact on airline behaviour. Finally, the strategies pursued by each flag carrier in response to both European liberalisation and US deregulation are analysed and evaluated in terms of their effectiveness. An insight into what Europe's restructured airline sector is likely to comprise by the turn of the century is contained in chapter 7.

Post-War Evolution of Western Europe's Airline Industry

Many people would regard the process of liberalisation of Western Europe's air transport industry as being a comparatively recent phenomenon. Whilst the European Commission's systematic approach in pushing Member States and carriers to accept the competition rules of the Rome Treaty[5] has been of crucial importance, pressure on governments to relax their regulatory policies has been evident for virtually the whole period of time the rules have been in place. Over the years charter carriers have been particularly adept at devising means by which to circumvent the regulations, effectively liberalising them. In many instances the implied spirit of the legislation has been flouted, whilst the precise wording complied with. Mounting public pressure for access to cheaper air transport generally has ensured that existing rules were not modified to nullify these actions. Rather ironically, the most blatant infringements have been perpetrated by none other than the scheduled carriers themselves, the intended beneficiaries of the protective regime. Governments have been forced throughout to give ground as a result of changing market conditions. As a consequence, liberalisation has been an on-going evolutionary process that has its origins long before the Commission became involved in the sector.

4.1 Establishing the Bilateral Regime

As in most other parts of the world, agreements concerning international airline services within Europe have been based on the exchanging of reciprocal traffic rights between individual States. The failure of the 1944 Chicago Convention to reach a consensus regarding the establishment of a multilateral system for the exchanging of international traffic rights resulted in this piecemeal approach.[6] The free market philosophy advocated by the US Administration was unacceptable to most other governments who were keen to nurture their fledgling air transport industries. The basic aim of the regulatory policy established by European governments therefore was to protect their scheduled, mostly publicly owned, flag carrying airlines from competition. By tightly controlling market entry on both domestic and international routes, countries were able to provide their national carriers, in nearly all instances the sole designated operator, with virtual monopoly power.

The precise terms of bilateral agreements have depended very much on the attitudes of the parties concerned. Some, such as those involving former Eastern bloc countries, have been of a highly restrictive nature, whilst others, particularly those based on the USA-UK Bermuda Agreement of 1946, have been liberal by comparison. The terms agreed between countries with flag carriers of comparable power and ability tended to be less restrictive than those contracted between a country possessing a small and relatively weak airline and one with a well developed and financially strong national carrier. An additional factor that has had an influence has been the granting of fifth freedom rights, which have required the agreement of third countries.[7] The precise details contained in bilateral treaties have seldom been made public as some of their more blatant anti-competitive features could well have provided political capital to those advocating a more laissez faire approach.[8]

Where international routes were concerned, the fact that two airlines ordinarily could be anticipated to be providing a service, given each country's right to designate their own nominee, would lead one to have concluded that some element of competition would be evident. In practice, any such possibility was eliminated by route licence holders colluding, a common manifestation of this being the pooling of revenue.[9] In many instances this situation continued well into the 1980s as table 4.1, which lists the twenty busiest intra-European routes in 1987 and their operating carriers, illustrates.[10]

4.2 The Effects of Tight Regulation

The result of this regulatory strategy was to create a scheduled airline industry which until comparatively recently remained in certain respects immune to competitive pressures. In the UK, where various attempts have been made since 1960 to introduce some degree of head to head[11] competition on domestic routes, it has been only since the mid 1980s that the avoidance of any harmful effects to the national airline has not been the predominant factor in such decision making. Even in 1991, multiple designation remained the exception rather than the rule on most intra-European routes.

Table 4.1 The 20 Busiest Scheduled Intra-European Routes in 1987

Route	Passenger Traffic	Carriers	5th Freedom Airlines
London-Paris	2,400,000	AF,BA,BR.	GF,IR,KU,MK,MH, PA,PK,SV.
London-Amsterdam	1,300,000	BA,BR,HN, KL.	AI,KU,MH,PK.
London-Dublin	1,200,000	BA,DA,EI.	
London-Frankfurt	1,000,000	BA,BR,LH.	CX,ET,GF,NW,MH, PA,PR,RG,TG.
London-Brussels	800,000	BA,BR,SN.	SV.
London-Zurich	750,000	BA,DA,SR.	AC,UL.
Copenhagen-Oslo	725,000	SK.	FI,NW,PA,SR.
London-Geneva	670,000	BA,BR,SR.	AI,KU.
Copenh'n-Stockholm	640,000	SK.	JU,NW,OK,SN.
Milan-Paris	550,000	AF,AZ.	TW.
London-Milan	540,000	AZ,BA,BR.	
Geneva-Paris	510,000	AF,SR.	AC,RK,TW.
Frankfurt-Paris	480,000	AF,LH.	AI,AR,AV,CX,PA, PK,TG.
Berlin-Dusseldorf	480,000	AF,BA.	PA.
Amsterdam-Paris	470,000	AF,KL.	GA,JL,KU,PR,RG.
London-Madrid	460,000	BA,IB.	
London-Rome	460,000	AZ,BA.	AI,ET,IR,KQ,PR.
Helsinki-Stockholm	450,000	AY,SK.	AF,PA,SR.
London-Dusseldorf	450,000	BA,LH.	AC.
Paris-Rome	450,000	AF,AZ.	CX,KU,RK,SV.

Source: ICAO Origin & Destination Survey for 1987; ABC World Airline Directory for July 1987.

The absence of competition resulted in inefficiency, necessitating high fares, these being set in relation to the costs of the least efficient operator on a route. This situation became readily more apparent in the late 1960s and early 1970s as a result of experience gained from both the US intrastate airline markets and, more

71

especially, from the relatively unregulated charter markets existing within Europe and across the North Atlantic. Economic regulations governing such operations traditionally have been much less restrictive than those constraining scheduled services. The Chicago Convention had left the authorisation of non-scheduled services to the discretion of individual states. This resulted in each country being required to give prior authorisation to inbound charter flights. Not surprisingly, a wide range of attitudes became apparent with some countries flatly refusing to authorise services not operated by their own flag carriers, whilst others, especially those keen to develop their tourist industries, adopted an 'open door' policy. In 1956 the 22 members of ECAC had agreed to mutually waive this requirement of prior authorisation[12], paving the way for the development of inclusive tour operations.

Despite this accord, the desire to protect the markets of scheduled carriers remained the key priority. Charter carriers were restricted to operating flights in which all the seats on an aircraft were taken by a single party, whether group, individual or organisation. The sale to the general public of individual seats on non-scheduled services was allowed only in the case of customers purchasing inclusive packaged holidays from authorised specialist tour operators chartering entire aircraft. In addition, regulatory authorities restricted the fares that could be charged for these packaged tours and the capacity that could be offered. For example, the UK's Air Transport Licensing Board stipulated that the minimum price for inclusive tours could not be less than the full scheduled airline fare to the same destination.[13] However, growing public demands for cheaper holiday travel and the realisation that the vast majority of charter flight traffic was newly generated resulted in these restrictions being gradually relaxed.

4.3 Breaking the Mould

The rapid growth during the 1960s in the package tour market to Mediterranean resorts and in North Atlantic affinity group charters[14] enabled a number of non-scheduled carriers to develop and acquire large fleets of aircraft. At first the type of equipment used for these operations were predominantly castoffs from the scheduled airlines, but by the early 1970s many companies were operating new jet-powered machines, similar to those used by the flag carriers. The second class image of non-scheduled services was slowly eroded so that by the mid 1970s, with the exception of seat pitch, in-flight service became virtually indistinguishable from that offered to economy class passengers on scheduled flights.

Growing affluence, longer paid holidays and a desire for sunshine provided a ready market for charter firms with their low cost product. The regulations that restricted the use of non-scheduled services to group only activities became increasingly circumvented. Clubs were established where the sole purpose was to avail members of cheap air travel. Requirements stipulating a minimum length of time before members became eligible to make use of charter flights organised by a club were openly flouted. The necessity to provide accommodation (a formal requirement for inclusive tour charter licences) also became subject to looser interpretation. To comply with the regulations accommodation of the most rudimentary kind was provided as part of the package, with its use never being seriously anticipated by any of the parties involved. Seat only charters ultimately became a natural extension of both the inclusive tour and affinity group businesses, enabling the general public to further bypass the regulatory controls. Under the contemporaneous regulations, scheduled operators were effectively priced out of these rapidly expanding markets as a result of their high operating costs.

4.4 Changing Scheduled Market Conditions

The markets of scheduled carriers were also subject to changes, some of which fundamentally altered their operating environments. The large increase in available capacity on many scheduled routes in the early 1970s, the result of the introduction of wide-bodied aircraft, forced carriers to find ways to increase demand. Attempts to reduce fares via normal channels were neither a sensible nor a feasible proposition. The priority was to preserve the amount of revenue derived from existing traffic levels whilst at the same time generating new business. Negotiating lower fares via the usual IATA traffic conferences, aside from being both time consuming and fraught with the problem of requiring the agreement of many carriers, would only succeed in adding weight to the growing voice of opinion that existing tariff levels were excessive. Although the regulations were specifically established to protect scheduled carriers, changing circumstances made it prudent for these same airlines to adopt the seemingly hypocritical position of staunchly advocating retention of the existing regulatory controls, whilst simultaneously actively infringing them by supplying tickets at below agreed rates to non-licensed agents. In effect, exploiting the rules in order to minimise any possible revenue dilution resulting from the newly introduced lower fares.

The need to fill larger aircraft also encouraged carriers to exercise their entitlements to fifth freedom rights, further exacerbating the problem of excess capacity. With the rapid growth of what has been euphemistically referred to as the bucket shop market, passengers acquiring their tickets via officially licensed travel agents at government approved fare levels became increasingly disgruntled.

Consumer pressure groups were established with the prime aim of securing a general reduction in fares. Partly to appease their higher fare payers and partly to reduce the revenue loss from their unofficial price discrimination policies, scheduled airlines began to differentiate the quality of service they offered their economy class passengers. The introduction of business class provided carriers with a highly profitable means by which to persuade users not to economise on the fares they paid.

The coexistence of these two seemingly incompatible attitudes to Europe's airline industry was maintained throughout the 1970s and for much of the 1980s. Initially governments were able to maintain this apparently contradictory approach because of the very different requirements of passengers using the two types of service. As figure 4.1 shows, most charter services catered to the needs of Northern Europe's holidaymakers whose main concern was to get to the resorts of the Mediterranean as cheaply as possible. By contrast, scheduled services were perceived primarily as providing essential links for business travellers. Over time this distinction became more difficult to justify. By the mid 1980s, immediately prior to the Commission's involvement in the sector, the actual market for airline seats in many Western European countries bore little resemblance to that intended given that regulatory controls were not rigorously implemented.

Table 4.2   Growth of Intra-European Non-Scheduled Passenger Traffic

Year	Non-Scheduled	% of Total Intra-European	% of Total RPKs
1975	25,500,000	40.2	52.5
1976	25,800,000	38.7	50.4
1977	28,100,000	39.0	49.4
1978	30,100,000	39.0	49.0
1979	33,300,000	40.1	50.1
1980	31,800,000	39.6	50.4
1981	32,300,000	39.3	50.3
1982	34,800,000	41.4	52.3
1983	37,500,000	43.3	55.0
1984	41,000,000	43.8	55.4
1985	42,000,000	42.9	54.6

Sources: ICAO Circular 200-AT/78, 1986; & ECAC Digests of Statistics.

Figure 4.1   **Main European Charter Traffic Flows**

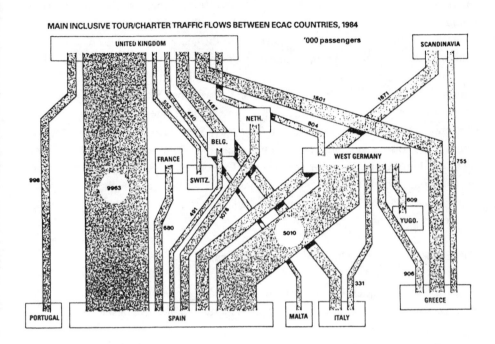

MAIN INCLUSIVE TOUR/CHARTER TRAFFIC FLOWS BETWEEN ECAC COUNTRIES, 1984

Source: Wheatcroft, S. & Lipman, G. (1986), Air Transport in a Competitive European Market - Problems, Prospects and Strategies, Economics Intelligence Unit Special Report, p. 24.

4.5 Influence of the European Commission

Despite the increasing involvement of the Commission it has continued to be individual governments and the main power groups within the industry itself that have dictated the speed and extent to which regulatory policy has been relaxed in Europe. National interests have been preserved wherever possible, with Community Policy often reflecting this. Nonetheless it has been the increasing power and influence of the Commission that has provided an important stimulus to the process of liberalisation.

It has been only comparatively recently though that this body has turned its attentions to air transport. In 1961 the Council of Ministers had exempted air and sea transport from the competition rules of the Rome Treaty until such time as a Community-wide policy could be developed. It was then not until the mid 1970s and a decision of the European Court of Justice that the general rules of the Treaty were applicable to maritime transport, that the Council of Ministers were forced into some action, albeit of a very limited nature. In 1978 it issued a list of priorities for air transport, but, given the vested interests of the Member States no reference was made to either market entry, capacity, or fares.[15] A year later, the Council set up a consultation procedure for dealing with third party States and established a directive concerning noise emission. That same year the Commission issued its first Memorandum dealing with air transport.[16] To help trace the involvement of the Commission, Council of Ministers, Court of Justice and other European organisations in the development of regulatory policy Table 4.3 provides a chronology of major relevant events.

Table 4.3   **Chronology of Significant Events**

1956   ECAC multilateral agreement on non-scheduled operations.

1957   European Community consisting of six member States established by the Treaty of Rome.

1961   EC Council of Ministers exempted sea and air transport from competition rules of the Rome Treaty until a policy could be developed.

1967   ECAC multilateral agreement on scheduled service tariffs.

1973   UK, Denmark & Ireland join EC.

1979   EC Civil Aviation Memorandum No. 1 published, which set out general objectives regarding air transport policy.

1980   EC introduce proposal to Council regarding inter-regional services.

1981   EC report on scheduled air fares within the Community published.

1982   US/ECAC Memorandum of Understanding introducing a multilateral agreement on non-intervention zones for North Atlantic tariffs. ECAC COMPAS Report on Competition in European Air Services published.

1983   EC Inter-Regional Air Services Directive issued by Council.

1984   EC Civil Aviation Memorandum No. 2 published, which advocated the harmonisation and liberalisation of intra-European bilaterals, and the introduction of competition rules with certain exemptions. UK/Netherlands liberal bilateral agreement signed.

1986   Nouvelles Frontieres case at European Court of Justice established that rules governing competition in the Rome Treaty applied to air transport.

EC introduce proposal to amend 1983 directive on inter-regional services.

ECAC Memorandum of Understanding, involving representatives of several States, on capacity share and tariffs but not market entry.

1987 EC Single European Act implemented, which makes unanimous approval of Council decisions no longer necessary, only a qualified majority.

Stage 1 of liberalisation approved by Council.

1988 Sorensen Plan discussed, which envisages the Commission gradually taking over responsibility for the Air Service Agreements of the 12 member States.

1989 Court of Justice decision in Ahmed Saheed case, declaring null and void ipso jure agreements on tariffs applicable to scheduled routes.

Stage 2 of liberalisation proposals put forward by Commission.

1990 Second aviation package approved by Council of Ministers.

1991 Commission publishes its third package of liberalisation proposals.

1992 Council of Ministers approves third stage measures.

Following the 1979 Memorandum, which set out a list of broad objectives for air transport and had the effect of increasing debate on this controversial topic, the Commission was asked by the Council and European Parliament in 1980 to prepare a report dealing with scheduled airline fares within the Community. This was published a year later and concluded that, in relation to costs, fares were not excessive, but suggested that procedures for tariff development could be improved. Later that year, to further this suggestion, the Commission proposed to the Council that they issue a Directive dealing with tariffs. At the same time the Council were asked to consider making a parallel regulation which would have the effect of making air transport subject to the competition rules of the Rome Treaty. A great deal of debate ensued regarding these proposals but the Council were unable to reach agreement. It would appear that too much was at stake! An exasperated European Parliament successfully brought the matter before the Court of Justice in a case which cited the failure of the Council to meet its obligations under the Treaty.

The Commission's other initial involvement concerned inter-regional air services, no doubt because they were regarded as posing the least threat to incumbents.[17] The fact that it took the Council three years to reach agreement on this matter, the terms of which were much more restrictive than originally proposed by the Commission, gives a clear indication of how reluctant many Member States were to altering the status quo. Not surprisingly the results of this directive were very limited, with the Commission reporting in 1986 that only 15 new routes had been approved under these provisions. Katz (1987) identified the directive's shortcomings as i) limiting... '..approval.. to services between the smaller airports', ii) being only applicable..'..to aircraft having less than 70 seats', iii) requiring a minimum distance of 400 kms, iv) that '..it did not apply if one of the two States concerned could demonstrate that the proposed new service is *already satisfactorily catered for* by existing direct services between the two airports..or if an indirect scheduled air service already exists between the airport concerned and another airport situated within 50 kms', and v) that..'..it did not provide for fifth freedom rights to carry traffic to third countries'. These extremely tight conditions, particularly the exclusion of category 1 airports, provided a clear insight as to where the Council of Ministers priorities lay. On a positive note however, the 1983 directive did at least represent the Community's first multilateral agreement on air transport.

Following this largely abortive attempt to move the Council in the direction of applying the Rome Treaty's competition rules to air transport, the Commission introduced its second Memorandum in 1984.[18] The main thrust of its recommendations were the harmonisation of existing bilateral agreements, with greater emphasis being placed on the use of market forces in the areas of capacity and fares, and the introduction of the Treaty's competition rules to this sector. The sensitive area of market entry was dealt with '..cautiously'.[19] As regards tariffs the Memorandum introduced the concept of zones of non-intervention or approval, as a means to circumvent governments failing to reach agreement on the introduction of innovative fares. In terms of the sharing of capacity it proposed rejecting a strict division in favour of a minimum 25% safeguard level for each of the two participants. As to the competition rules the aim was to apply Articles 85 to 90 for an initial seven year period to intra-Community routes only, with the possibility of exemptions being granted by the Commission.

Reactions to the proposals varied in accordance with inherent vested interests. The Council established its own working party to consider how the recommendations could be implemented. The outcome of these deliberations were in the form of a report and a list of guide-lines, which were endorsed by the Council in December 1984.[20] Whilst the guide-lines appeared to reduce the extent to which the Commission's full recommendations could be implemented, they did in the words of Wheatcroft and Lipman .. '..suggest a growing political realisation of the need for the Community to take action in respect of tariff, capacity and competition before possible Court decisions severely constrain the scope of action available'.[21] Minds were not sufficiently concentrated on this possibility however, as a consequence the core issue concerning the application of the Treaty's competition rules was left to the judiciary to determine. This they did in what generally has been referred to as the Nouvelles Frontieres case.[22]

The French Tribunal de Police had taken the Nouvelles Frontieres case to the European Court as they were considering taking criminal action against airlines and travel agents who were selling tickets below government approved levels. A key question posed by the French authorities concerned whether or not the system by which its government approved tariffs ran counter to the competition rules of the Rome Treaty. The Court's response was that such a regime at the time of its deliberations did not contradict the rules, but that this situation could change if the Commission or Member States deemed otherwise. Of critical importance however was the Court's clear decision that the competition rules did apply to the air transport sector. Whereas before the Commission had had little scope to push Member States in the direction of agreeing a multilateral policy aimed at removing barriers to competition, they were now in a position to be able to force the Council to do this. This was because until such time as the body of Ministers approved a regulation dealing with competition, they were empowered to determine which collusive practices were legal and which were not. It began to exercise this power after the Council failed in June 1986 to reach formal agreement both on capacity and tariff liberalisation and on the drafting of a regulation dealing with competition.

The Commission wrote to a number of the Community's scheduled airlines giving them two months to terminate certain activities which it reasoned to be in contravention of Article 85 of the Rome Treaty. The most publicised example of this concerned the matter of Aer Lingus providing a financial inducement to KLM to dissuade the latter from operating a service to Dublin.[23] Additional pressure was exerted by the Commission which threatened to withdraw its proposals on group exemptions from the competition rules unless the Council arrived at a sensible conclusion by June 1987. It would seem reasonable to conclude that it was these various actions that persuaded the Council's Ministers to adopt a more liberal approach. By agreeing regulations which implemented the competition rules they were able to minimise any damage to their respective national airlines. The alternative lay in the Commission using the European Court to outlaw anti-competitive practices, which would effectively have removed the influence Ministers could have exercised in this regard. Hardly surprisingly, within the twelve months stipulated by the Commission the Council were ready to unanimously agree a package initiating such regulations. However, final agreement was delayed a further six months after Spain's last minute veto over the matter of access to Gibraltar.

The liberalisation measures agreed in December 1987 consisted of two regulations implementing the Rome Treaty's competition rules and two other measures aimed at relaxing the restrictions on fares, capacity and entry. As regards the competition rules, Articles 85, which prohibits anti-competitive agreements, decisions and concerted practices, and 86, which prohibits abuse of a dominant position to affect trade between Member States, became effective. The precise activities which were considered as contravening these principles were not defined however. Many of the collusive practices then employed by scheduled operators, such as the pooling of revenue, limiting of capacity and agreeing of fares, were clear breaches of Article 85. To facilitate the reaching of an agreement a number of block exemptions were included in the Council's package, providing immunity for many of these activities for a three year period.

The measures agreed in December 1987 concerning tariffs, market access and capacity are summarised in Table 4.4. These at first glance convey the impression of substantial change, but as one commentator concluded in mid 1988 ..'..they have been confined to the smaller airlines and markets, mostly involving UK and Irish airlines and destinations. The heartland of Europe's air transport industry - the major flag carriers and the prime inter-hub services - remains largely untouched.'[24] Ireland, Luxembourg, Netherlands, and the UK had liberalised their respective bilateral arrangements well in advance of policy recommendations issued by the Commission. Market entry to intra-European routes in the latter part of the 1980s was largely the result of these liberal reciprocal agreements, rather than any overall Community policy.

Table 4.4   Measures Agreed by the Council of Ministers in 1987

Capacity

Controlled on a country-pair basis. From January 1988 to September 1989 capacity may be adjusted within the range + to - 5% of an equal share. From October 1989 this is increased to + and - 10%. Services operated under the terms of the 1983 inter-regional agreement are excluded from this calculation.

Market Access

Multiple designation is compulsory on a country-pair basis and, under the following conditions, on a city-pair basis:

i) During 1988 on routes which in 1987 had at least 0.25 million passengers;

ii) in 1989 the preceding year's minimum traffic level is reduced to 200,000, with the addition of an alternative constraint stipulating the minimum number of flights on a route during 1989 at 1200;

iii) in 1990 this is further reduced to 180,000 in terms of passengers and 1000 with regards to flights.

Fares

Still required to be filed with each country with not more than 60 days advance notice. Automatically approved if not disapproved by one State within 30 days. They must be approved if reasonably related to long term fully allocated costs.[25]

Automatic approval for the following:

i) discount fares of 60-90% of the normal economy fare;

ii) deep discount fares of between 45 and 65% of the normal economy fare

iii) super discount fares down to 10% below the lowest approved fare under conditions relating to length of stay and advance purchase.

Source: 'The EEC's New Air Transport Package', Frere Cholmeley, 1988.

For its part the Commission regarded the 1987 package as an important first step on the road to securing an internal market for air transport. 'The Commission naturally would liked to have achieved even greater liberalisation in this first phase, but was willing to settle for the agreed package on the basis of a commitment by the Council to adopt, by 30 June 1990, further measures of liberalisation with a view to the completion of the internal market by 1992' (Nicholas Argyris, Division Head in the Directorate General for Competition, February 1988.)[26] As regards the impact of this first phase of Community action, the Transport Commissioner Karel van Miert expressed the package to be ..'proving a modest success'. However, although several new routes had been established between hub airports and regional centres (and in a few instances, newly acquired fifth freedom rights exercised) no downward pressure had been exerted on normal economy fare levels. In addition, France and Italy had shown themselves to be reluctant to fully implement the 1987 agreement.

It was clear from the proposals published by the Commission in July 1989 that they were keen to overcome the various shortcomings of the first package of measures and push ahead as much as possible with liberalising the bilateral arrangements existing between Member States. Table 4.5 summarises their proposals to the Council. In certain respects their task was made easier by the actions of the Court of Justice. The Ahmed Saeed case[27] (which resulted from a Frankfurt travel agency being served a writ at the behest of Lufthansa on account of having sold discounted tickets obtained outside of West Germany) established that the imposition of a single price policy forced upon carriers by an airline holding a dominant position would contravene Article 86 of the Rome Treaty. This applied not only to intra-Community services, but also to domestic services and those involving third party countries. The Court also declared that Member States approving tariff agreements between airlines either abusing a position of dominance or operating a cartel would be in contravention of Article 86. In addition, recourse to Article 90, which would allow some respite from this ruling on the grounds of public service, would require... '..clear details as to the nature of the mission and its effects on the structure of the prices schedule.'[28]

Table 4.5   The European Commission's Second Package Proposals

----

Fares

i) In place of the existing regime a double disapproval requirement is proposed. Fares would be automatically approved if not disapproved by the relevant authorities at each end of a route. Fare changes of greater than 20% would require detailed examination by Member States.

ii) Fifth freedom carriers to be allowed to act as price leaders.

iii) Proposals to apply to domestic services and those to third countries.

Capacity

i) The present 60:40 sharing arrangement between States is recommended to increase to 67.5:32.5 from October 1990 and to 75:25 from April 1992. It is also proposed to allow a further 5% increase in capacity share if airlines from one Member State have reached the upper limit of the range.

ii) It is proposed that the Commission could suspend the above extension to the capacity sharing proposals if a Member State's airlines were suffering serious financial difficulty.

iii) All inter-regional services to be excluded from capacity calculations.

iv) The seating limit for services between hub and regional airports should be raised to 100.

Market Access

i) Multiple designation limits to fall to 180,000 passengers, or 1000 return flights, per year from January 1990. Further reductions are proposed for introduction in January 1991 (140,000 passengers or 800 return flights per annum) and January 1992 (100,000 passengers or 600 return flights).

ii) Existing airport derogations, excluding those involving the Greek Islands, to be phased out, resulting in the establishment of third and fourth freedom rights between all other airports open for intra-Community international services.

iii) Member States would no longer have complete discretion to refuse one of their own carriers from operating any intra-Community or domestic route. A State could only refuse a licence if the route applied for did not meet its published criteria of economic viability, which must exclude any detrimental impact on existing operators.

iv) A Member State would be obliged to accept a third or fourth freedom service licensed by another Member State and operated by one of its carriers, except under circumstances in which an aircraft seating more than 100 passengers is proposed for operation on an inter-regional route on which a new service utilising equipment with less than 100 seats had been established during the previous three years. Exemption could also be obtained by applying to the Commission if it could be deemed that an airport had insufficient facilities, navigational aids or slots.

v) Member States could continue to regulate in a non-discriminatory way the distribution of traffic between airports forming part of a system in a particular locality.

vi) As regards fifth freedom traffic rights it is proposed that Community airlines be allowed to exercise such rights within the Community as an extension of a service from, or as a preliminary of one to, their State of registration, with no exclusion for hub airports. This would be subject to a limit of 50% of a route's annual seat capacity, but would not apply to aircraft equipped with fewer than 100 seats. A change of gauge would be permitted on such services. Such operations would be only subject to the approval of the third country concerned.

vii) Sixth freedom services would be allowed as it is proposed that carriers be allowed to combine third and fourth freedom flights through their home airport using the same aircraft and flight code.

viii) It is advocated that cabotage be permitted with the following provisos: firstly, that the service should be an extension of, or preliminary to, a third or fourth freedom service; secondly, that at least one of the airports served is a regional airport; and thirdly, that not more than 30% of the annual seat capacity may be utilised for the carriage of domestic passengers.

Source: 'Summary of the Commission's Proposals for 1990', UK Dept. of Transport, September 1989.

The measures agreed by the Council of Ministers in June 1990 followed on directly from their deliberations the previous December at which they had appeared to have changed tactics. Somewhat surprisingly a recommendation was approved that they should adhere to many of the Commission's proposals. A clear distinction was drawn however between the regulations that were to be in force pre January 1993 and those thereafter. In essence, the gradual process of easing the existing regulations was to be continued until the end of 1992, with changes of a more substantive nature being left for implementation until at least January 1993. It would appear from this that whilst the Ministers were continuing as usual to put off the evil day, they were at least acknowledging that at some point in the not too distant future they would have to bite the bullet!

Overall the policy of gradually easing the restrictions contained in existing bilateral agreements has resulted in greater freedom in the determination of fares, an increase in the number of routes which have a multiple designation of airlines and fewer restrictions on the capacity that operators are able to provide. In its third package of proposals published in July 1991, the Commission wanted to see the rapid introduction of 'cabotage' throughout the Community with very few exceptions. Cabotage, the freedom for any EC owned and registered carrier to enter any intra-European city-pair market it so desires however, will not be a reality until 1997. The attitude of the Association of European Airlines (AEA), the organisation representing the interests of Europe's major scheduled carriers, on this matter has been a major factor behind the delay in its implementation. Their views were made clear in a white paper on air transport and the internal market presented to the Chairman of the Commission in June 1991.[29] In the majority of cases the support of their respective governments on the matter of cabotage can be assumed to have been automatic. Table 4.6 provides a brief summary of the Commission's proposals.

Table 4.6   The Commission's Third Package of Liberalisation Proposals

---

Capacity

Removal of capacity constraints on all routes with the exception of those with a traffic volume of less than 30,000 seats per year.

On these low trafficked routes access is to be limited in one of two ways, either in allowing just one carrier to operate or by restricting the seating capacity of aircraft that may be utilised (80 seats).

In the event of financial hardship caused to a carrier by an over provision of capacity, the Commission will undertake an investigation which may result in constraints being imposed.

Market Access

Fifth freedom rights and cabotage to be fully implemented from January 1993. (The Commission however acknowledged right from the outset that cabotage was likely to prove a highly controversial matter and that its implementation could well be delayed.)

Special provision to be granted for essential services to development areas that are uneconomic to operate. Also for unprofitable interregional services.

Inter island services in the Azores and Greece are to be exempted from these recommendations for a ten year period.

Fares

A 'double disapproval' regime to be implemented for a three year period from January 1993.

All controls on fares to be lifted from January 1996.

A fares appeals procedure is to be implemented on routes with less than 30,000 seats supplied per annum, those operated under public service obligations and those with only one or two carriers present.

Source: H. Nuutinen (1991), 'Third Package Proposals', Avmark Aviation Economist, July/August, pp. 2-3.

As is clear from table 4.6 existing constraints on pricing policy and capacity have also been recommended for rapid removal by the Commission in their latest round of proposals. In many respects their earlier recommendations on these two matters have been more conservative than that already existing between a number of the more liberally minded Member States. Much debate has ensued about the Commission's third package of recommendations, but in June 1992 the Council of Ministers reached agreement on the proposals, albeit in modified form. As has been apparent for a long time now, the kind of deregulation with safeguards that the Commission favours is unlikely to be a reality before the latter part of the 1990s. Long before then Europe's most powerful flag carriers will have succeeded in exerting a controlling influence over any competition they could conceivably be expected to face.

4.6 The Strategic Response of Airlines

Europe's scheduled carriers have had the considerable advantage over their US counterparts of being able to observe which strategies have proved to be the most effective in countering the effects of full scale deregulation. One of the key tactics employed by US carriers to defend themselves against competitors, the reorientation of their essentially linear route systems to hub and spoke operations, was already a feature of Europe's air transport. Each flag carrier has always had its routes centred on a single hub, invariably its country's capital city. Unlike in the US, the position of dominance at each hub has been maintained through restrictions placed on market entry by the relevant regulatory authority. With the prospect of this protection being removed, flag carriers formulated their own defensive tactics. A number of distinct strategies have been employed by airline managers, reflecting what each has perceived best suited their particular company's strengths and weaknesses. Not surprisingly, over time these have evolved partly to suit changed market conditions, partly to counter the regulatory efforts of the Commission and partly to reflect a greater insight on the part of management, all to some degree the outcome of deregulation policies being pursued in other areas of the world.

Most defensive strategies usually involve the elimination or neutralising of potentially powerful competitors. This prospect has only really existed in two Western European countries in which there has been a scheduled airline operating of sufficient size to pose such a threat to the flag carrier, namely France and the UK. In the former case, UTA with its experience of long haul operations could, if it had been acquired by or merged with another major European airline, have formed a formidable challenge to Air France, as market entry to routes previously denied it became a possibility. In the UK, British Caledonian with its base at Gatwick initially posed the greatest potential threat to British Airways (in much the same way as UTA did to Air France) by making it possible for a prospective interloper to gain access to runway slots and terminal space in its home territory. The flag carrier's base at Heathrow was at this stage subject to a ban on additional carriers using it, effectively providing the company with some degree of protection from competition. Birmingham airport, another possible point of access for a powerful competitor, was tackled by the firm through its part acquisition (since terminated) with Maersk[30] of The Plimsoll Line, owners of the then Birmingham Executive Airways. Its part purchase of the Plimsoll Line also provided it with the potential to counterattack SAS in its most important home territory. Its failed attempts to obtain a shareholding in Sabena, in conjunction with KLM, were aimed at achieving a geographical dominance at the main traffic generating western edge of Continental Europe.

A first approach involved consolidating a position of dominance in one's home territory, either through the acquisition of other scheduled carriers or by engaging these companies to operate scheduled services on the major's behalf. Most independent operators have been made in some way dependent on their country's flag carrier. Some operate feeder services to the national airline's traffic hub, whilst others provide service on regional routes with more appropriately sized and configured aircraft than the flag carrier would wish to undertake. In other instances carriers, whilst not being operationally dependent on their country's major carrier, have simply recognised the futility of competing head to head against such an overwhelmingly powerful adversary and have simply kept their heads down!

A rather unusual case is that of KLM, a carrier with a disproportionately large international route network in comparison to its small home market. To maintain such a global system it has been vitally dependent on getting passengers and freight originating or destined for other European countries to travel via Amsterdam. This has been achieved through the partial acquisition of scheduled operators in other States, Air UK being a prime example.

Links between the major European flag carriers have only very recently started to develop beyond the alliance stage. A number of cooperative ventures have been formed, but most have been of a very tentative nature rather than any full blown attempt at combining resources. The British Airways and KLM attempt to effectively take over Sabena by not meeting with the approval of the Commission may have had the effect of making carriers somewhat wary of proceeding rapidly in this direction. Appendix 3 provides a detailed summary of the European Airline Industry.

4.7 Summary

The fundamental essence of the European Common Market is that the economic barriers existing between Member countries by virtue of their different nationalities should be eliminated. It had been envisaged that by the beginning of 1993 the defences provided by each State to safeguard its interests would have been dismantled and replaced by a collective system designed to promote the affairs of all Members. Any attempt though to create a single market comprising a group of nations with such a wide and diverse range of economic and political philosophies can realistically only be expected to proceed at snail's pace.[31] This certainly has been the experience of the current twelve Member States, with the European Commission acting as a sort of group conscience - reminding governments of their obligations with respect to the implementation of the Rome Treaty. Unfortunately each of the Member States has sought to use the Union to pursue their own idiosyncratic objectives, and rather than conveying a picture of increasing harmony it is conversely much more a case of nations continuing to vie with one another, much as before.

Attempting to force States to accept the responsibilities implicit in their membership has not been an easy task. Numerous delaying tactics have been employed when an individual State has perceived that its best interests are not likely to be served. Whilst some individuals have seen the light and wholeheartedly accepted the doctrine of a common market, in the main the same cannot be said of their governments.[32] It would be unrealistic to think that 'Europe's interests' are likely to have been foremost in the minds of those responsible for devising the strategy of their country with regards to this issue. The day that the average Frenchman, Italian, or Spaniard regards himself firstly as a European and only secondly as a native of his country of birth has yet to dawn. Finding a balance between attempting to push ahead with the implementation of ideas enshrined in the Treaty of Rome concerning competition and also acknowledging the reality that the main players are primarily concerned with pursuing their own individual best interests (which will often imply a contrary objective) is the exceedingly difficult task of the European Commission.

The benefit of having the experience of economic deregulation in the world's largest airline market has made the European Commission acknowledge the essential role of antitrust legislation. To prevent a similar outcome in Europe the Commission is seeking to limit anti-competitive behaviour through the adoption of such laws. In the future, prospective mergers are to be evaluated in terms of their likely impact on competition, with those that are adjudged as being anti-competitive being barred. Such decisions invariably will provoke controversy and considerable debate given the undoubtedly clear conflict of interest between what the Commission would regard as being best for consumers, namely a strongly competitive environment, and that which would serve most the objectives of flag carriers. Given the strong concerns of Governments regarding the latter it is likely that much watering down of the Commission rulings can be anticipated, as has been the case in the past. Operating an effective antitrust policy will be a far from easy task, especially given the strongly partisan interests of the Member States.

Notes

1. The following 22 countries are members of the European Civil Aviation Conference (ECAC): Austria, Belgium, Cyprus, Denmark, Finland, France, Germany, Greece, Iceland, Ireland, Italy, Luxemburg, Malta, Netherlands, Norway, Portugal, Spain, Sweden, Switzerland, Turkey, UK and Yugoslavia. This grouping of States is the most pertinent where matters of air transport are concerned.

2. Nuutinen, H., 'Charter Airlines in Europe', Travel and Tourism Analyst, November 1986, pp.19-20.

3. These charter carriers mostly form part of vertically integreted organisations, with inclusive tour operation being their primary activity.

4. In the mid 1980s the five largest airlines based in the European Community, British Airways, Air France, Lufthansa, KLM and Iberia, controlled some 68% of total traffic. Source: Association of European Airlines (AEA), Aviation Week, 9 March 1987.

5. The Treaty of Rome, signed in 1957 by the governments of Belgium, France, Italy, Luxembourg, Netherlands and W.Germany, established the European

Community. The primary aim was to remove any barriers to trade existing between the Member States in order to create a 'Common Market'. The six were joined by Denmark, Ireland and the UK in 1973, by Portugal and Spain in 1987, and by Greece in 1989. The Community, as established, is a supranational body with its own legislative, judicial and administrative powers. The first of these powers is exercised by the Council of Ministers, comprising ministers from each Member State, the presidency of which rotates on an alphabetic basis every six months. Judicial powers rest with the Court of Justice, made up of eleven judges assisted by a number of advocates general. The administrative function is performed by the Commission, consisting of 14 Commissioners nominated by Member States, but remaining independent of them. To perform its role the Commission has a secretariat of 19 directorates general, two of which, number IV dealing with competition and number VII concerned with transport, have the most concern with airline services.

6. In 1944 a Conference involving some 52 Allied nations had been called in Chicago to discuss the possibility of achieving a multilateral agreement with regard to the development of international airline services.

7. Fifth freedom rights provide a carrier with the ability to carry passengers and freight to and from a location in a country to which it ordinarily operates and a city in a third State. For example, United Airlines are able to operate scheduled services from London (Heathrow) to Amsterdam, Frankfurt, Hamburg, Munich, and a number of other European destinations under the terms of the US/UK bilateral agreement.

8. Bilaterals usually contain confidential 'Memoranda of Understanding' or 'Exchange of Notes', which specify in more detail particular aspects of the agreement.

9. Pooling has been used as a means by which a State with a weak carrier could gain some assurance that it would obtain an equitable share of the traffic carried and revenue earned on an international route. Doganis, R. (1985), Flying Off Course: The Economics of International Airlines, George Allen & Unwin, p. 29.

10. In 1982 ECAC found that two thirds of European bilaterals had no limit on the number of the number of airlines that could be designated. In practice though only 8% of city-pairs had more than one airline per State. Source: Katz, R. (1987), 'Liberalisation of Air Transport in Europe', Travel & Tourism Analyst, March, pp. 7-8.

11. The term 'head to head' refers to operations between the same two airports. An early example of this form of competition on UK domestic routes was provided in the early and mid-1960s by British Eagle, which was licensed to operate in

competition with British European Airways on the Glasgow route from Heathrow.

12. European Civil Aviation Conference (1956), 'Multilateral Agreement on Commercial Rights of Non-scheduled Air Services in Europe', Paris.

13. Wheatcroft, S. & Lipman, G. (1986), Air Transport in a Competitive European Market - Problems, Prospects and Strategies, Economics Intelligence Unit Special Report, p. 26.

14. Members of clubs and associations alledgedly travelling for a common purpose were able to charter aircraft. Minimum periods of time were stipulated before a new member was able to avail him or herself of the cheap travel opportunities offered by the club. As time past the rules controlling affinity group charters became increasingly infringed.

15. Council of Ministers (1978), 'Priorities in the Field of Air Transport', European Community.

16. European Community (1979), 'Civil Aviation Memorandum No.1 - The Contribution of the European Communities to the Development of Air Transport Services'.

17. 'Inter-Regional Air Services', Council Directive, European Commission, July 1983.

18. European Community (1984), 'Civil Aviation Memorandum No.2 - Progress Towards the Development of a Community Air Transport Policy'.

19. Wheatcroft, S. & Lipman, G., supra note 13, p. 51.

20. European Community (1984), 'Report of High Level Group to the Council of Ministers'.

21. Wheatcroft, S. & Lipman, G., supra note 13, p. 54.

22. European Court, April 1986.

23. Katz, R. (1987), 'Liberalisation of Air Transport in Europe', Travel & Tourism Analyst, March, p. 11.

24. French, T. (1988), 'So Far, So What?', Airline Business, August, pp. 16-19.

25. In earlier discussions within the Commission the idea that fares should be reasonably related to the costs of an efficient operator had been put forward. However, the idea of efficiency was anathema to many States and the concept consequently was dropped.

26. Argyris, N. (1988), 'Competition in European Air Transport - The Role of the European Commission', Symposium of Air Law Group of the Royal Aeronautical Society on 'Airline Competition and the Treaty of Rome', London, 25 February.

27. The Ahmed Saeed case was brought before the European Court in May 1987 and related to a Lebanese travel agent who had bought discount tickets in

Lisbon for flights to Tokyo on Lufthansa services routed through Frankfurt. The fact that he was selling the tickets in West Germany had produced this test case.

28. Aeropa (1989), 'The Court of Justice of the European Communities "breaks" the System of Air Tariff Agreements', Brussels, April.

29. AEA, 'White Paper on Air Transport and the Internal Market', June 1991.

30. British Airways and Maersk each have a 40% shareholding in The Plimsoll Line, owners of Brymon and Birmingham European. These latter two carriers are soon to be merged adopting the name Brymon European.

31. Developments in Eastern Europe, particularly the rapid unification of Germany, are likely to add further delay to this process of harmonisation.

32. 'Eurocrats' working for the Commission tend to develop a different perspective than their fellow countrymen.

Bibliography

Katz, R. (1987), 'Liberalisation of Air Transport in Europe', Travel & Tourism Analyst, March, pp. 7-8.

5 Deregulation in Canada and Australia

The pressure faced by governments to deregulate their scheduled airline industries has been a worldwide phenomenon. Canada and (more recently) Australia have followed the US example in removing the majority of economic controls relating to their domestic markets. One exception to this policy has been the very lightly populated Northern region of Canada which, because of the perceived social necessity of its air transport services, remains tightly regulated. In both countries the respective regulatory authority had exerted a tighter control than had the Civil Aeronautics Board in the US. Despite each country sharing a number of similar characteristics, such as their huge land masses and small populations, the development of their airline industries has followed along very different lines.

Political factors have played a key part in determining how each country's air transport industry was allowed to evolve. In Australia the desire of the post-war Labour Administration to have their domestic airline services operated by a nationalised carrier set the foundations for the Two Airline Policy, introduced in 1957. In Canada the combination of strong regional governments and the designation of the nationalised flag carrier by the Federal Government as sole provider of transcontinental services ensured a strong demarcation in service provision. The manner in which these two airline industries have evolved under tight economic control is outlined below. The response of incumbents to deregulation is analysed and the restructuring process discussed.

5.1 The Impact of Economic Regulation on Canada's Airline Industry

In many respects the rapid restructuring of Canada's air transport industry into a duopoly following deregulation returned the sector to the point to which it had evolved during forty years of tight economic regulation. This earlier period had seen scheduled service provision gradually develop from a situation in which all trunk and international routes were operated by one state owned airline, Trans Canada Airlines, to one in which two carriers, Trans Canada and Canadian Pacific, competed on the former and shared the latter. The protection given by the Federal Government to Trans Canada Airlines had been extended over time to incorporate the privately owned Canadian Pacific. A consequence of this was that operators of regional services were prevented from encroaching on the markets of this duo. Some respite was provided latterly to these airlines in the form of freedom to engage in charter service operations, with the proviso that their core activities remained the provision of regional services.

In 1937 the Canadian Federal Government had established Trans Canada Airlines as a Crown corporation in order to develop transcontinental air services. The carrier continued as sole supplier of these trunk routes until 1959, when the Conservative Administration allowed Canadian Pacific (known as CP Air from 1968) to operate a single daily return flight between Montreal and Vancouver. Gradually the capacity constraints on CP Air's trunk operations were lifted, but it was not until 1978 that they were removed altogether. The key priority had been to secure the financial wellbeing of the Crown carrier. To this end the routes operated and fares charged by the Trans Canada (known as Air Canada from 1965) were controlled directly by the Federal Cabinet, unlike all other air transport carriers.[1]

As had been the case with the transcontinental routes, Trans Canada Airlines initially had been given a monopoly of international services, but in 1948 Canadian Pacific was designated the country's flag carrier in the Pacific. The privately owned airline's scheduled route network was extended considerably in 1965 when the Federal Government adopted a two airline strategy for its international service provision.[2]

Many regional carriers had been established in the early post war era. Their function was clearly delineated in a 1966 policy statement, which required them to supplement the trunk activities of the two national carriers but to in no way compete against them.[3] Under this amended policy regional airlines were allowed to operate domestic charters for the first time, with the proviso that this did not lead them to change their core business activity. The operation of International charter services was seen as providing good opportunities for this group of carriers. Their roles were further clarified in 1969 when a Ministerial policy statement stipulated the geographic locations in which the five regional operators were to focus their operations. These were as follows: Eastern Provincial Airlines (the Atlantic provinces), Nordair (the majority of Ontario and N.W. Quebec), Pacific Western Airlines (British Colombia and W. Alberta), Quebecair (the majority of Quebec) and Transair (the Prairies and N.W. Ontario).

By 1979 the regulatory regime governing domestic service provision had altered little from its inception aside from the fact that CP Air had been allowed to compete with Air Canada on transcontinental routes. Growing pressure for a change in regulatory policy from the electorate, partly the result of US deregulation, led to a comparatively rapid and fundamental transformation in government attitudes during the early part of the 1980s. Table 5.1 summarises the major policy initiatives that resulted.

Table 5.1   Moves Toward Canadian Deregulation

1979   All capacity limits on CP Air's transcontinental operations lifted.
          Wardair allowed to operate domestic advanced booking charters.
1984   The New Canadian Air Policy announced. The country was divided into North and South regions. The former was to be tightly regulated as before, but in the latter entry and exit conditions were relaxed with no restrictions on lower fares. Anti-competitive activities by Air Canada restricted.
1985   'Freedom to Move' Policy issued. Near full deregulation proposed.
1988   The National Transportation Act of 1987 became law. North/South distinction, with the latter having only few restrictions on pricing and market exit.

5.2 The Impact of Deregulation on Canada's Domestic Markets

By the time that Canada's domestic airline markets were being prepared for deregulation a good deal of evidence was available from the US as to the strategies that best suited a large incumbent carrier. One of the key requirements was the need to provide a large network of feeder services to a major airline's main traffic hubs. A major characteristic of US deregulation had been the development of code-sharing alliances between the major carriers and regional commuter operators. The realisation that except under extraordinary circumstances the financial viability of smaller airlines depended on their being able to provide a complementary service to their larger counterparts was readily apparent by the mid 1980s. The rapid absorption of Canada's regional carriers by Air Canada and CP Air stemmed directly from this restructuring experience south of the border. Table 5.2 traces the consolidation of Canada's scheduled operators as the industry prepared itself for near full scale economic deregulation.

Table 5.2   Consolidation of the Canadian Airline Industry

Carrier   1979 1980 1981 1982 1983 1984 1985 1986 1987 1988 1989 1990 1991

Trunks   **Majors**
Air Canada---Air Canada
                                                                                                Air Alliance
                                                                                                Air BC
                                                                                                Air Nova
                                                                                                Air Ontario
                                                                                                NWT Air

CP Air--
                                                    ↑   ↑   ↑   ↓
Regionals   ↑ ↑   ↑   ↓
Pacific Western----------------------------------↑---------↑------CAI-------------Canadian A/l Int.
                        ↑   ↑   *Air Atlantic*
Eastern Provincial--↑--------------------   ↑   ↑   *Calm Air*
                        ↑   ↑   *Inter-Canadien*
Nordair-----------↑----------------------- ↑   ↑   *Ontario Express*
                    ↑   ↑   *Time Air*
Quebecair-----------↑---------------------------------
                        ↑
Transair--------------↑
(Carriers shown in *italics* operate feeder flights on behalf of the two major carriers.)

Charter   **Charter**
Wardair---
                                                    Air Transat-------------Air Transat
                                                             ------Canada 3000
                                                    Minerve----------------
                                            Nationair-----------------------------------Nationair[*]
                                                            ([*]ceased trading 1993)
Worldways--

New Entrant

                                            City Express-------------------------------------

96

Immediately prior to the phase of consolidation Air Canada had over 50% share of the total airline market. By contrast CP Air was less than one half the size of the state owned carrier, with the four regional carriers trailing a long way behind.[4] To survive in a deregulated environment it was clear that CP Air would need to grow and become of a similar size to Air Canada. Over the following three years (1984-1987) this became a reality as CP Air acquired a controlling interest in a number of regional carriers. In 1984 Eastern Provincial and its affiliate Air Maritime were purchased. A year later the airline gained control of a second regional carrier, Nordair. In the following year 1986 it acquired Quebecair through its subsidiary Nordair Metro and took a 35% shareholding in Air Atlantic. The most important stage in this process of creating a carrier of comparable size to Air Canada came in December 1986 when CP Air itself was purchased by PWA Corporation, owners of Pacific Western, largest of the regional airlines. The two carriers became merged in 1987 when the name Canadian Airlines International (CAL) was adopted. A yet further increase in size came in 1989 when CAL bought out Wardair, the largest and most successful of Canada's charter airlines. Wardair had been the only significant market entrant following deregulation, but its low fares policy resulted in all three airlines incurring substantial losses on their domestic operations, though a lack of financial resources to sustain this strategy resulted in its subsequent swift demise.

Despite the rapid consolidation of the industry to a duopolistic structure, when compared with any of the US megacarriers Air Canada and CAL remain very small. Given the size of Canada's population it seems unlikely that two major indigenous airlines can ultimately survive. The recent poor financial performances of the two companies represents the clearest manifestation of this reality. In practice, aside from the possibility of one of the carriers declaring itself bankrupt, it has been inevitable for some long time now that only two other courses of action were feasible. Either the two could merge and form a single Canadian flag carrier or each company would have little choice but to join forces with a US airline. The first of these two options would most likely mean the effective takeover of CAL by Air Canada. Strong political objections to a scheduled airline monopoly irrespective of the fact that Air Canada was privatised in the late 1980s, would on past experience have made this the least likely outcome.

For a time the scenario incorporating US carriers showed some signs of materialising with American's announcement in January 1992 of its intention to acquire a 49% shareholding in CAL. In the event the deal was abandoned by American. Following this the two Canadian carriers began exploring the possibility of merging and after some differences of view finally agreed to a merger in September 1992. In the event the proposed merger did not take place. Subsequently, the two carriers have gone their separate ways, with Air Canada acquiring a 29%

shareholding in Continental and American continuing with its earlier intention to acquire a stake in Canadian, providing the latter was able to divest itself of its commitment to the Gemini CRS. This outcome may well prove to have been the better result for Canadian travellers, as prospects for competition are likely to be greater given two carriers, albeit no longer fully home grown.

5.3 Australia's Idiosyncratic Brand of Economic Regulation

As has been the case in Canada, politics have played a key role in determining the regulatory environment in which airlines have had to operate. The two key features of the Australian airline industry in the post war period have been the total separation of international and domestic operations and the adoption of a 'Two Airline Policy' covering internal interstate services.

In 1946 Australia's post-war Labour Government had wanted to nationalise the country's largest domestic carrier, Australian National Airways (ANA), but had been unable to do so as a result of a constitutional challenge. Instead they embarked on establishing an alternative state-owned airline, Trans Australia Airlines (TAA). By subsidising their company's operations the government enabled TAA to grow at the expense of ANA. However, a change to a Conservative administration in 1949 ultimately resulted in the evolution of a 'Two Airline' Policy, which was to become the hallmark of the Australian aviation scene for more than three decades. The underlying rationale of the policy was that two airlines competing against each other would produce a better result than if the market was monopolistic.

During the early and mid 1950s a number of carriers, notably Ansett, had been able to compete with ANA and TAA on the country's main trunk routes. ANA fared badly as a result of this competition and was eventually taken over by Ansett in 1957. The latter had agreed to take over the ailing company on the condition that the government introduced tight route entry controls. In an agreement unique to the airline industry, the government entered into a legally binding agreement with Ansett to enforce a duopoly in the supply of domestic airline services. Government imposed entry barriers prevented prospective competitors from gaining access to the interstate markets. In order to ensure that Ansett and TAA were and would remain of roughly equal size and strength, the Australian Administration rigorously enforced its controls over the importation of aircraft. This policy also had the effect of preventing potential competitors from acquiring the necessary hardware to mount a meaningful challenge. Table 5.3 provides a summary of the developments in regulatory policy.

From 1960 the 'Two Airline Policy' ensured the survival of both Ansett and TAA. Throughout the following three decades the two companies accounted for between 85% and 90% of total domestic demand.[5] The only other airlines operating scheduled passenger services were considerably smaller, functioning as regional carriers. Most of these companies have since been acquired by Ansett, as table 5.4 illustrates.

Table 5.3   Developments in Australian Regulatory Policy

1946	Trans Australia Airlines set up by Labour Government.
1951	Conservative Administration announces intention to establish a 'Two Airline Policy'.
1957	Ansett acquires ANA on condition of regulatory protection.
	The 'Two Airline Policy' era begins.
1979	Domestic Air Transport Review published by Dept. of Transport.
1981	Holcroft report into domestic air fares published. Independent Air Fares Committee set up.
	'Two Airline Policy' modified and extended for a further five years. Three years notification of policy termination announced. Majority of rationalisation measures abolished.
	Air freight market deregulated.
1986	May report on domestic airline economic regulation published.
1987	Government gives formal notice to end the 'Two Airline Policy'.
	East West Airlines acquired by Ansett.
1990	Deregulation of domestic interstate routes.
	Compass Airlines commences operations.
1991	Government announced intention to fully privatise Australian and partially privatise Qantas (49%).
	Compass ceases operations.
1992	International Air Services Commission established.
	Labour Administration announced plans to merge Australian and Qantas. Full privatisation to follow by mid 1993 (since delayed until 1995).

The bulk of the demand for airline services within Australia is accounted for by a small number of high density trunk routes. The remainder consists of a large number of low density markets catered for by both the two trunk operators and regional airlines. Given the difficulties involved in operating very low trafficked routes these have increasingly been handed over to the regional companies. During the 'Two

Airline' era overall demand increased only gradually, with normal economy fares remaining much the same in real terms.[6] As in the US and Western Europe, the proportion of passengers travelling on discounted fares increased. By 1985 some 42% of passengers were using discount fares.

Table 5.4   Consolidation of Australia's Domestic Airline Industry

Carrier   1979 1980 1981 1982 1983 1984 1985 1986 1987 1988 1989 1990 1991

Trunks

Trans Australia A/l---------------------------------------Australian-----------------Australian
(Eastern Australia
Southern Australia
Sunstate)

Ansett-- Ansett
(Ansett Express
Ansett WA
Eastwest)

Regionals

Ansett A/l of New South Wales------------------------Air NSW--------------Ansett Express

A/l of N Aust'lia-----------------------Ansett NT(ceased trading 1991)

Ansett A/l of South Australia---------------(ceased trading 1986)

MMA--------------A/l of W Australia-----------Ansett WA----------------------- Ansett WA

East-West--(acquired by Ansett in 1987)----Eastwest

Air Queensland---------------------------------------(ceased operations 1988)

New Entrant

Compass------

(Compass A/l commenced operations in December 1990 and was declared bankrupt twelve months later. The assets of Compass were acquired by Southern Cross A/l, another prospective new entrant, which intended to reactivate Compass using five MD-80 aircraft in 1992. This second attempt also ended in failure in March 1993.)

Earlier concerns with creating an environment in which the two carriers would actively compete against other were dropped. By the early 1960s rationalisation of the services operated by the two companies became the major concern. A considerable degree of collusion took place between Ansett and TAA during the 1960s and 1970s, directly encouraged by government through a body called the Rationalisation Committee. Growing public concerns about the provision of airline services led to a number of reviews into the industry in the late 1970s. Comparisons made between fares charged on international routes and those on internal services of a similar journey length revealed wide disparities. A major outcome of these criticisms was the discouraging of collusive activity. As a consequence, since 1980 the two airlines have increasingly competed in such areas as in-flight service, frequency, departure time, and availability of discount fares. An additional competitive pressure faced by Ansett and TAA during the early and mid 1980s came from the regional carrier Eastwest. It had attempted to gain access to a number of trunk routes, but given the long term nature of such a venture it posed no immediate threat to the duopolists. In any event the airline was acquired in 1987 by Ansett.

5.4 Australia's Experience with Domestic Deregulation

As has proved the case in many countries, public interest in the general removal of economic controls grew during the 1980s. The decision to deregulate the country's domestic airline passenger services was not however announced by the government until October 1987. A further three years then elapsed before the change could be implemented, the result of a condition imposed in earlier legislation. In 1981 the 'Two Airline Policy' had been extended for a further five year period (1982-87), with the possibility of the government formally terminating the contract but only after giving three years notice to so do.

The aim of the 1987 policy was to remove all existing constraints on entry to interstate routes and on the capacity provided.[7] The one exception to this freedom concerned the operators of international services who were to be excluded from supplying the domestic market. This requirement represented a partial continuation of existing policies under which Qantas held a virtual monopoly of international passenger services but was prohibited from operating internally. To facilitate other airlines entering the interstate markets import controls on aircraft were to be lifted. Existing controls on fares were also to be removed, giving carriers complete freedom in pricing their services.

By the time deregulation came into effect in November 1990 only one of the many prospective new entrants had actually materialised. Compass Airlines began operations a month later on the country's main trunk routes using a small fleet of 280 seat Airbus A300-600R aircraft. Formed by former employees of Australian (the name adopted by TAA in 1986), the carrier expected its operating costs to be only 50% of its two rivals. The problem of gaining sufficient access to terminal space at the country's major airports was cited by the new entrant right from the outset as a major factor prohibiting effective competition.[8] In the event Compass survived for just over a year. Problems of under capitalisation, access to essential infrastructure and the operation of aircraft that were too large for the job in hand brought about the company's swift demise. At the time of writing none of the other prospective companies have commenced operations, with attempts to reactivate Compass using smaller capacity aircraft also having proved unsuccessful.

In the light of the failure of Compass, major changes to aviation policy were announced by the Australian Government in February 1992. These involved the proposed formation of a single aviation market with New Zealand and the opening up of international markets to Ansett. This change in government thinking followed an earlier decision to privatise the two state owned carriers, Qantas and Australian, but to keep separate their ownership and operations. This latter requirement however was amended as part of the change of policy announced in February 1992. Cross-shareholdings between the two airlines were now to be permitted.

Since then aviation policy has undergone further amendment with the Government deciding that Qantas be allowed to acquire Australian and that the combined company be fully privatised by the middle of 1993 (since delayed until 1995). Closer cooperation between an enlarged Qantas and the New Zealand flag carrier is inevitable, given the 20% shareholding that Qantas has in Air New Zealand. In the light of this strong likelihood it is difficult to see Ansett having a very secure future, despite it being allowed to operate internationally for the first time. Overall it is difficult not to conclude that these comparatively rapid amendments to policy stem from the swift demise of Compass, the lack of other serious interstate market contenders and the increasing consolidation of the airline industry worldwide.

Notes

1. The regulation of Canada's airline industry has been undertaken by, in chronological order, the Board of Transport Commissioners (1938-44), the Air Transport Board (1944-67), the Air Transport Committee of the Canadian Transport Commission (1967-87), and since 1988, the National Transportation Agency.

2. Canadian Pacific was designated flag carrier for scheduled services to Asia, Australia, New Zealand, Latin America and Southern Europe in 1965.

3. Oum, T. H., Stanbury, W. T. & Tretheway, M. W. (1991), 'Airline Deregulation in Canada and its Economic Effects', Transportation Journal, Summer, p. 5.

4. Oum, T. H., Stanbury, W. T. & Tretheway, M. W. (1991), supra note 3, p. 9.

5. Forsyth, P. (1991), 'The regulation and deregulation of Australia's domestic airline industry' in Button, Kenneth (editor), *Airline Deregulation: International Experiences*, David Fulton Publishers, p. 50.

6. Forsyth, P. (1991), supra note 5, p. 51.

7. Interstate routes account for the majority of Australia's domestic traffic. The regulation of intrastate routes remain the preserve of individual states. Western Australia had already opted for deregulation prior to the national government's announcement.

8. Long term leases of 20 years had been agreed between the airport authorities and the two incumbent airlines before deregulation occurred.

6 Evolving attitudes to economic regulation

It has been the failure of specific markets to produce and allocate goods efficiently, together with wider social and strategic objectives identified as being in the public interest, that has provided the rationale for the economic regulation of industry. Traditionally, economists (such as Bator, 1958), have distinguished two main sources of market failure, namely: the abuse of market power by firms operating under conditions of monopoly and oligopoly and the presence of externalities, both resulting in a distortion of market forces. In addition to these, asymmetry in the availability of information to do with prices and product quality has been increasingly regarded as forming a major source of market failure.[1] Other motives for adopting economic regulation have been such issues as unemployment, the strategic importance of industries, and income redistribution. In the case of many of the transport industries, aspects of safety and financial instability encouraged governments to introduce economic controls. As regards distributional objectives, concern centred on achieving a more equitable balance of income and wealth, but, as Kay and Vickers (1988) have argued, these are matters that are better left to more efficient instruments of public policy.

The earliest preoccupation of governments in the matter of market failure concerned attempts at preventing monopolistic firms from exploiting their market power. Given that many such industries, particularly the utilities, exhibited the presence of substantial economies of scale, attempts aimed at fragmenting such natural monopolies could only result in less efficient production. Given the fundamental desire to protect consumers interests, the only sensible option lay in directly controlling the behaviour of such firms. Regulatory authorities were established as a consequence, with each given a remit to make a particular industry operate in such a manner as to satisfy the public interest.[2] In order to extend consumer protection to encompass all markets, the US Administration introduced antitrust legislation in 1889.[3]

This attitude of safeguarding the public was later widened to include situations where it had been adjudged that competition had become overly excessive. As a consequence, regulatory authorities were established with remits to limit entry to such markets. For example, in the case of the UK bus (local stage carriage) industry the 1930 Road Traffic Act[4] established a system of route licensing, which was aimed at eradicating the poor standards of safety and financial instability experienced in the 1920s. Similar motives were behind the establishment of equivalent regulatory agencies to control the airline industries in both the UK and US.[5]

Economic regulation therefore has been used by Governments to attempt to control the amount of competition that firms face in particular markets.[6] In situations which revealed the presence of insufficient competitive pressure intervention aimed at introducing greater rivalry. In the main this was attempted by the altering of market structure, but if this proved infeasible attention was focused on constraining the behaviour of firms in such a way as to replicate the effects of the desired level of competition. In a similar manner adjustments could be made if it was adjudged that excessive competition was preventing the public interest being served in a particular market. Constraining behavioural conduct has usually involved the establishment of limitations on prices, product quality, distribution and information disclosure. For example, prior to nationalisation railway companies in the UK were forced to publish their rates for the carriage of freight, enabling road hauliers to undercut them.[7]

The ever-widening net of government controls, partly the result of regulatory authorities extending their areas of control [what Peltzman, (1977) refers to as creeping regulation] and partly arising from an extension of legislation to incorporate markets not previously controlled, such as health and the environment, made economists start to question the wisdom of having such an extensive system of constraints. Prior to 1960 a normative, non-quantitative approach prevailed, with regulation being perceived as an essential guard against inefficiency and exploitation. The view that economic regulation could be counter-productive and did not always work in the interests of consumers originated from a study of the electricity generating industry in the US by Stigler and Friedland (1962). That regulation of natural monopoly public utilities in the US had not produced any significant impact on their operating behaviour was expressed by Jordan (1972). Stigler (1971) postulated the theory that regulatory authorities had been captured by the firms that they had been formally charged with regulating and had adopted policy accordingly. This was extended by Peltzman (1976) into a general theory in which regulation is portrayed as being a commodity which can be bought and sold like any other. In this theory regulators are assumed to provide a cartel management service which can be purchased by interested parties, predominantly producers. This view has particular pertinence to US markets, where antitrust legislation precludes the possibility of collusive activities between firms.

The prevalent view amongst economists by the early 1970s was one of overkill in terms of the extent of market regulation. The consensus verdict was that a considerable improvement in efficiency would result if markets were substantially deregulated. Many economists expressed the view that regulatory measures either had failed to achieve their goals, or had actually produced a worse situation for consumers. Jordan (1972, p.176), for example, made the strong assertion that

> Regardless of the diverse aims and hopes of the consumers, industry leaders, and legislators who brought about the extension of regulation over various industries, the actual effect of such regulation has been to protect producers. It follows that wherever substantial monopoly power exists in a non-regulated market structure, regulation should have relatively little impact; and, where there is little or no monopoly power in the prior market structure, regulation should have an important impact by helping formerly independent producers form a cartel for their benefit and protection.

Prior to the emergence of the 'capture' theories an important, yet highly erroneous, assumption was that regulation had been imposed at relatively little cost. Posner (1974) explored this viewpoint and contended that in reality 'the costs of regulation probably exceed the costs of private monopoly'. If this outcome has generally been true, then it must constitute a fairly damning indictment of economic regulation. That it could be so inefficient and counter-productive can have stemmed only partly from an inability to adapt and develop policy to fit changing circumstances. Niskanen (1971), for example, argued that regulators were essentially bureaucrats who sought to maximise their budgets, and so have objectives that conflict with the original intentions of those who established the regulatory framework.

That any type of government intervention carried with it the inherent risk that the proposed cure might produce a worse outcome than that which it was designed to eradicate had been clearly established by the early 1970s. Changing circumstances could render a set of once relevant regulatory policies outmoded and anachronistic. The more rigidly these controls were enforced the greater the likelihood of this occurring. Once a set of rules and guidelines became established, resistance to further change could occur. Even those firms which adapted their operations in a positive spirit of compliance had sought means to exploit their regulators. In the US, regulation had provided firms with a cartel management service that under normal circumstances would not have been possible given the antitrust laws.

By the mid 1970s in the US the pendulum had swung full measure and come to rest firmly in the direction of complete economic deregulation. One of the main advocates of this policy, Alfred Kahn, had the opportunity to oversee the dismantling of a complete regulatory authority, the Civil Aeronautics Board, together with all of its rules.[8] That this relatively extreme viewpoint had become conventional wisdom is symptomatic of the relatively abrupt and dramatic reversals of public policy that are widely observed. A belief in the inherent competitiveness of markets was an essential requirement for exponents of such a policy. Although as Kahn has argued both before deregulation (1978) and more recently (1988), one could always fall back on antitrust legislation if such faith turned out to be misguided. For those however whose faith had a tendency to waiver and were in need of further convincing, the arrival of Contestability Theory in the early 1980s provided additional persuasion in this matter.

The Theory of Contestable Markets, developed by Baumol, Panzar and Willig (1982), provided an essential catalyst in this reforming process, switching attention from the actual competitive environment within a market to a wider preoccupation with the ease with which other firms could enter. The more contestable a market the greater the influence of potential entrants on the decision making of firms operating within that market. In such markets established firms could be expected to set price at such a level so as to discourage entry. The greater the contestability, the nearer this price level would be to that which could be anticipated if the market were operating under conditions of perfect competition.

Invariably, firms that operate in unregulated markets will be engaged in devising and perfecting means by which to limit access to prospective competitors, utilising all their collective ingenuities in the process. By contrast, firms operating within the protected environment of the highly regulated industries will have no need to expend time and money on such pursuits. Besides freeing firms to operate in markets of their own choosing, deregulation involves them, possibly for the first time, in the onerous and costly task of protecting themselves from rivals. Their first priority in these circumstances assuming that they act rationally, would be to explore as quickly as possible the scope that exists for establishing such protection. The really vital question therefore as to whether it makes sense to completely deregulate a particular industry depends critically on the extent to which previously regulated firms are able to establish effective entry barriers. Basing one's expectation of this on the prior performance of these firms would be unrealistic, to say the least. Industries exhibiting some degree of similarity and not operating under highly regulated conditions would be likely to provide a much more accurate indication of this.

That the type and extent of regulation generally employed came to be regarded as being surplus to requirements can be attributed to three main causes, namely: changed circumstances, the capture of regulatory authorities by producers and the bureaucratic self-interest of regulators. No one theory of regulation provides a sufficiently comprehensive explanation as to why this situation had emerged. What is clear is that when industries were first regulated the primary concern had been with eradicating specific market failure swiftly and radically. This meant that attention had been too narrowly focused, with little or no consideration being given to longer term implications. Policy in the main had been too inflexibly applied, with the result that regulators were intransigent, not adjusting policy in response to the often substantial changes that had occurred in the competitive conditions prevailing in industries within their jurisdiction. This seemingly heavy handed and unsophisticated approach arose primarily because of the way in which change in public policy is realised. The sudden and relatively abrupt changes of government policy in matters of market intervention reveal that all too often little, if any, serious thought has been given to long term direct and indirect consequences.

The problem of sustaining an optimum level of competition within dynamic and often rapidly changing markets in such a way as to satisfy all participants is no more likely to be forthcoming by the removal of all economic controls than it is by adopting any other type of blanket approach. In general, the more concentrated an industry the greater the likelihood that it will be necessary to impose restrictions on firms wishing to merge and on those engaging in collusive practices in order to limit consumer exploitation. Market concentration is determined predominantly by the extent of economies of scale and scope[9] and the ease with which incumbent firms are able to erect other forms of entry barrier. If collusion is likely to be a significant feature of an industry then invariably it will be necessary to impose standards on the conduct of firms, or, as in the US, ban the activity altogether. Comparisons with similar industries in the home country or, if this proves impossible, using relevant examples from abroad, would provide a valuable insight into what is most likely to occur, as Peltzman (1977) has argued. Fixing maximum concentration standards that are to be universally applied may be unnecessarily cumbersome and inefficient. For example, the imposition of a 25% maximum market share for each firm may be entirely apposite in certain instances, but not in others. Flexibility is a fundamental requirement in any type of market intervention. The need to recognise that substantial change can occur rapidly in the competitive conditions prevailing in a market is essential. Rigidity of thought whether the outcome of political dogmatism or arising from a desire to maintain a neat and uniform approach needs to be avoided at all cost. That a government will never get it quite right is not in question!

Notes

1. For example, Salop & Stiglitz examined situations in which consumers were badly informed about prices; whilst Akerlof examined the market for secondhand cars in the US to explore the question of information in connection with product quality. (Salop, S. and Stiglitz, J. (1977), 'Bargains and Ripoffs: A Model of Monopolistically Competitive Price Dispersion', Review of Economic Studies. Akerlof, G. (1970), 'The Market for Lemons: Qualitative Uncertainty and the Market Mechanism', Quarterly Journal of Economics.)
2. The first federal regulatory commission in the US, the Interstate Commerce Commission, was established in 1887.
3. The Sherman Antitrust Act was passed by Congress in 1889, with the principle objective of preventing constraints being applied to competition.
4. The effects of the 1930 Road Traffic Act are discussed by Gwilliam, K. M. and Mackie, P. J. (1975) in Economics and Transport Policy, George Allen & Unwin, pp. 302-6.
5. The Civil Aeronautics Authority was set up in 1938 by the US government to regulate pricing and entry on interstate routes, determine mail rates and control all aspects of safety. It adopted the title Civil Aeronautics Board in 1940. The Air Transport Licensing Authority was established by the UK government in 1938 to adjudicate over a system of formal hearings for the allocation of subsidy and route licences.
6. Button argues that regulatory policy concerned with market failure has been aimed mainly at making firms perform as if they were operating under conditions of perfect competition. Button, K. J. (1986), 'New Approaches to the Regulation of Industry', The Royal Bank of Scotland Review, p. 19.
7. Gwilliam, K. M. and Mackie, P. J., supra note 4, pp. 22-7.
8. Alfred Kahn was Chairman of the Civil Aeronautics Board from 1977 to 1982.
9. Economies of scope and density have played an important part in determining concentration levels in the scheduled airline industry.

Bibliography

Bator, F. (1958), 'The Anatomy of Market Failure', Quarterly Journal of Economics.
Baumol, W. J., Panzar, J. C., and Willig, R. D. (1982), Contestable Markets and the Theory of Industry Structure, Harcourt-Brace-Jovanovich, San Diego.
Jordan, W. A. (1972), 'Producer Protection, Prior Market Structure and the Effects of Government Regulation', Journal of Law and Economics, Vol. 15.

Kahn, A. E. (1978), 'Kahn Urging CAB Deregulation Drive', Aviation Week & Space Technology, 6 March, pp. 35-39.

Kahn, A. E. (1988), 'Surprises of Airline Deregulation', American Economics Association Papers and Proceedings, pp. 316-22.

Kay, J. A. and Vickers, J. S. (1988), 'Regulatory Reform in Britain', Economic Policy.

Niskanen, W. (1971), Bureaucracy and Representative Government, Aldine-Atherton, Chicago.

Peltzman, S. (1976), 'Toward a More General Theory of Regulation', Journal of Law and Economics, Vol. 14, pp. 109-148.

Peltzman, S. (1977), 'The Gains and Losses from Industrial Concentration', Journal of Law and Economics, Vol. 20, pp. 229-63.

Posner, R. A. (1974), 'Theories of Economic Regulation', Bell Journal of Economics and Management Science.

Stigler, G. and Friedland, C. (1962), 'What Can Regulators Regulate: The Case of Electricity', Journal of Law and Economics.

Stigler, G. (1971), 'The Theory of Economic Regulation', Bell Journal of Economics and Management Science, Vol. 2, pp. 3-21.

7 Prospects for competition in a global marketplace

In a paper delivered to the Royal Aeronautical Society in London in March 1992 the Chairman of United Airlines, Stephen Wolf, argued that competition would continue to remain a feature of the scheduled airline industry despite increasing levels of market concentration. Whilst this seems a reasonable assertion, it is expectations about the extent and nature of the competition that are of more crucial concern. Deregulation unleashed a considerable amount of competitive pressure on US carriers in their domestic markets, much of it emanating from low cost new entrants to the interstate markets. Substantial gains in efficiency resulted from this competition forcing the former trunk carriers to reorganise and reduce their operating costs. Average fares fell in real terms and demand for airline services doubled over a decade.

These highly competitive conditions have as yet not abated. The process of US airline consolidation has still to run its full course. The protection of bankrupt companies provided by US Chapter 11 legislation has enabled a number of financially defunct carriers to survive. Consumers have benefited considerably from the fare wars that this has encouraged, but the outcome for suppliers during downturns in the economic cycle has been massive financial losses. Only one major carrier, America West, now remains operating under these artificial conditions. In the longer term competition between the four or five ultimate survivors is likely to be a much more controlled and stable affair than the comparative hysteria of recent years. Rivalry will occur, but it is difficult to imagine many situations in which one megacarrier would continue to slog it out with another of its kind for very long. Undoubtedly different perceptions will exist about the prospects that a competitive action might produce, but as the deregulated airline market becomes more mature these are likely to grow fewer with time.

7.1 The Quest for International Traffic

The restructured US airline industry poses a considerable threat to carriers worldwide. The ability of the few surviving and financially sound US carriers to fully develop their domestic hub and spoke route systems has enabled them to extract considerable economies of scope and density. Having exploited most of the benefits that this strategy can offer internally, these companies have been keen to build on this sound base by developing extensive international networks. Table 7.1 lists the transatlantic and transpacific routes acquired by the three largest US carriers from their weaker rivals since 1985. Non-US registered carriers being denied the benefits of extensive domestic feeder networks are placed at a considerable disadvantage. In addition, the extensive fifth freedom rights held by US airlines worldwide has provided them with opportunities to develop hub operations abroad. For many reasons carriers based in other parts of the globe have been unable to obtain the level of benefit derived by their US competitors from hub and spoke route networks.[1]

Table 7.1   Transatlantic and Transpacific Route Transfers by US Carriers

Transfer Date	Original Operator	Acquiring Carrier	Route(s)
1986	Pan Am	United	All Pacific Operations
1990	TWA	American	London-Chicago
1991	TWA	American	Heathrow-New York Heathrow-Los Angeles Heathrow-Boston
	Pan Am	United	Heathrow-Chicago Heathrow-Los Angeles Heathrow-Miami Heathrow-New York Heathrow-Washington
	Continental	American	Seattle-Tokyo
	Pan Am	Delta	Remainder of Pan Am's Atlantic Operations
1992	TWA	USAir	Gatwick-Baltimore Gatwick-Philadelphia
	America West	Northwest	Honolulu-Nagoya

Major European carriers derive the major part of their profits from long haul operations. As a consequence, international route expansion by powerful US airlines poses a serious problem. There is a similar threat from Far Eastern flag carriers who also have been keen to expand their international networks. The entry to long haul scheduled operations of a number of non-flag carrying airlines based in the Far East, such as Asiana Airlines (South Korea) and EVA Airways (Taiwan), has exacerbated the situation.

In response to this increasing challenge, several medium-sized carriers have rationalised their international operations. By developing route sharing alliances with other airlines they hope to be able to compete in as cost effective a manner as possible with the rapidly growing international networks of the successful US megacarriers and their Far Eastern counterparts. Air Canada's strategy of jointly operating routes with other small and medium-sized airlines provides a good example of this type of approach. The ability of these carriers to operate independent international services on other than their most heavily trafficked routes will diminish as the megacarriers further establish their global networks, whether in their own right or in tandem with others.

It would appear from the above that small and medium sized carriers are likely to become increasingly dependent for their survival on a comparatively small number of megacarriers. In the medium term this latter group is likely to find that the formation of collaborative ventures with each other provides an easier and more cost effective means to access international traffic outside of their usual spheres of influence. The recent wave of global alliance development involving many of the world's largest carriers is explored in the updated section following chapter 10. The ability of small and medium-sized carriers to provide efficient feeder services for these powerful consortia will to a large degree dictate their futures. The likelihood of smaller nations being able to continue subsidising their loss making flag carriers will diminish as more international traffic is lost to these dominant airlines.

7.2 Defending One's Own Back Yard

Preventing carriers from other countries acquiring medium-sized scheduled airlines based in one's own territory, particularly those operating international services, has formed a key part of the defensive strategy of several major European flag carriers. Access to slot constrained airports has been a particular focus of attention in this regard.[2] The competitive threat faced by British Airways from British Caledonian Airlines (BCAL) was not great whilst the carrier remained independent, but had the valuable assets under BCAL's control been acquired by a powerful rival, this would have posed a considerable problem to the flag carrier. Similarly Air France faced a potential dilemma with UTA.[3]

The tying in of locally based small and medium-sized scheduled airlines has been a tactic employed by many of Western Europe's flag carriers. The approach adopted by Air France, for example, has involved the airline contracting other carriers to operate services on its behalf. TAT and Brit Air have been two notable beneficiaries of this policy over the past decade. Making potential rivals dependent in this manner has been an approach adopted by several European flag carriers.

More recently, an increasing trend has been for the dominant carrier to become a part owner of the smaller airline, thereby enabling the former to exert a greater degree of influence over the latter. In a few instances flag carriers have acquired complete ownership of such companies. Table 7.2 lists the locally based feeder companies owned by the major European flag carriers. The requirement imposed by the European Commission on Air France to divest itself of several international and domestic routes and its shareholding in TAT in order for it to gain approval to acquire UTA, has not resulted in a rapid upsurge in competition. In such circumstances 'biting the hand that feeds you' would hardly seem a sensible cause of action to follow. Directly challenging the flag carrier may not appear a particularly attractive proposition, especially if a complementary role is on offer. It is certainly possible to take, or even drag, a horse to water, but making it drink - well that is another matter!

Table 7.2   European Flag Carriers' Ownership of Local Airlines

Country	Major Carrier	Secondary Airline	% Ownership
Austria	Austrian	Austrian Air Services	100
Belgium	Sabena	Delta Air Transport	49
		Sobelair	100
France	Air France	Air Charter	80
		Air Inter	72
Germany	Lufthansa	Condor	100
		Lufthansa Cityline	100
Greece	Olympic	Olympic Aviation	100

Country	Major Carrier	Secondary Airline	% Ownership
Ireland	Aer Lingus	Aer Lingus Commuter	100
Italy	Alitalia	ATI	100
		Avianova	100
		Eurofly	45
Netherlands	KLM	KLM Cityhopper	100
		Martinair	30
		Transavia	80
Spain	Iberia	Aviaco	33
		Binter Canarias	100
		Binter Mediterraneo	100
		VIVA Air	96
Sweden	SAS	SAS Commuter	100
		Scanair	100
Switzerland	Swissair	Balair/CTA	57
		Crossair	48
United Kingdom	British A/w	British A/w Regional	100
		Brymon	100
		Caledonian	100

7.3 Gaining Access to New Markets

The most recent development in this area has involved cross border acquisitions. The third and final stage in the liberalisation of Europe's airline services should theoretically at least provide carriers based in any of the twelve member state countries with the option of operating any route they choose. Acquiring control of an established carrier provides an easier and better basis for entry into what previously were foreign markets. The acquisition by British Airways in 1992 of a 49% shareholding in the German regional carrier Delta Air (since renamed Deutsche BA) provides a good example of this trend. Table 7.3 provides details of the cross border shareholdings held by European flag carriers.

Table 7.3   Cross Border Acquisitions by European Flag Carriers

Flag Carrier	Acquired Airline	Country of Registration	% Ownership
Aer Lingus	Futura Int.	Spain	25
Air France	Austrian	Austria	1
	CSA	Czechoslovakia	40
	Sabena	Belgium	37
British A/w	GB A/w	Gibraltar	49
	Deutsche BA	Germany	49
	TAT	France	50
KLM	Air UK	United Kingdom	15
	Delta A.T.	Belgium	29
Lufthansa	Austrian	Austria	10
	Lauda Air	Austria	26
SAS	British Midland	United Kingdom	40
	Spanair	Spain	49
Swissair	Austrian	Austria	10

7.4 Going Global

The extent to which the industry will become globally integrated is as yet unclear. Whilst there have been a number of moves in this direction, some more tentative than others, a wholehearted shift has yet to be observed. The additional benefits that a full global linkage could confer to participating airlines over looser collaborative ventures may well prove to be small. Many of the cost advantages that accrue from large size do not necessitate carriers working in tandem to be in effect a single entity. Similarly the ability of three or four loosely aligned carriers to generate revenue may well not be significantly enhanced through a closer bonding. All is dependent on there being a strong commonality of purpose. If the interests of carriers seeking to collaborate with each other are not sufficiently close, then ultimately either the weaker will be absorbed in furtherance of the interests of the more powerful or the participants will go their separate ways to seek more amenable associates. Given sufficient of a common purpose existing between those collaborating then the eventual emergence of a dozen or so tightly integrated giants will be most likely. If this is not the case, then a much more varied mix of collaborative ventures will be apparent. Powerful factors involving the preservation of nationalistic aspirations would tend to make the latter possibility the more likely.

7.5 Implications of Globalisation

Conventional wisdom concerning the economics of operating an airline has fundamentally altered as a result of deregulation. The various production economies that can be derived from operating large integrated hub and spoke route networks, particularly those of scope, are only fully exhausted at very large levels of output. The result in the US is an industry dominated and controlled by a handful of very large carriers. Given that the total European air transport market represents some 52% of the US domestic market, it would not seem unreasonable to anticipate the existence of only three, or possibly four, consortia accounting for the vast majority of intra-European traffic by the end of the decade.

The degree of competition then likely to exist between these European-based megacarriers may bear some resemblance to that which now exists in the US. As has been apparent there the minimum number of operators required to produce a satisfactory competitive environment is not at all obvious. Much has depended on the aspirations of the individual participants and on the nature of their commercial relationships. In certain city-pair markets the presence of just two carriers has resulted in sufficient pressure to maintain both efficient production and fares that do not generate near monopoly profits. However, in other duopolistic markets the benefits of greater productive efficiency have not been shared with consumers. (A tacit understanding on behalf of the two parties that fare competition would be unlikely to prove mutually attractive rather than any covert attempt at collusive action probably provides the best explanation for such behaviour.)

It is expectations about the choices that consumers are likely to be faced with in the future that is at the heart of the debate about the longer term effects of deregulation. Inefficiency, high fares and the limited choice available to the users of scheduled airline services were the major reasons for liberalising economic controls. The formation of alliances, as with any other form of collusive action, is likely to result in less competitive pressure. Whether the degree of competition thence remaining would be sufficient to produce the range of choice that consumers would regard as being acceptable is of fundamental importance in this matter.

If global consolidation occurs on a wide scale and is allowed to continue unabated by those charged with regulating the airline industry as is stated above it is quite conceivable that only a dozen or so consortia would ultimately supply most world demand for air transport. As in the domestic US market, competition would continue to feature, but it would be unlikely to be of the type or to the degree envisaged by those that advocated deregulation. At present airline passengers travelling longer distances within the US experience a greater degree of choice than those making shorter trips. Given further consolidation of US carriers this trend is likely to become even more apparent. The former group of travellers have the possibility of routing via the hubs of different airlines, whilst for the latter, aside from some very high density routes with more than two carriers offering service, competition mainly stems from other modes of transport. This is also increasingly likely to be the case in Europe if the industry is allowed to consolidate to the level desired by the larger carriers. In these circumstances an extended European high speed rail network may well provide the main competitive threat in the future to the few remaining scheduled airlines based in the region.

Whilst it is true that much of the competitive pressure experienced by the US airline industry resulted from new entrant carriers (and latterly from companies operating under Chapter 11 bankruptcy protection), the real innovators have been the larger incumbent carriers. These companies have demonstrated considerable degrees of skill and imagination in accessing clientele and extracting revenue. Transformed into lean and efficient marketing led giants, it would seem inconceivable that these companies will relax in their efforts to remain alert and dynamic organisations. As yet the industry has not achieved the rates of return on invested capital that are typically earned in other industrial and service sectors. The longer term expectation of airline shareholders and management is for this gap to narrow and ultimately disappear. Increasingly senior airline managers are being recruited from other sectors, their expectations and benchmarks gained in companies earning healthier financial returns from capital.

In the longer term it would seem apparent that competition from a comparatively small number of worldwide players will be sufficient to keep the airline industry lean and efficient. An important benchmark will be provided by the financial returns gained in other sectors. As a consequence, airline shareholders are likely to gain a greater share of the benefits of the improved efficiency that results from deregulation, thus further reductions in average real fares would appear most unlikely. Old style cartels are unlikely to return, but in certain respects the degree of control that surviving consortia will be able to exert over their markets will give the appearance of such. Choice will exist, but governments may well need to match the industry by tackling regulation on a global scale if the interests of consumers are given too low a priority by a more stable and mature airline industry.

Notes

1. Within Europe a number of factors have contributed to limiting the effectiveness of a hub operation. These have included congested air space, limited access to takeoff and landing slots at major airports, and ill-designed passenger terminals that cannot be adapted for hub operations.

2. Despite the enormous technical advances that have affected the air transport sector over the past two decades a critical constraining factor remains the fundamental requirement for the use of conventional runways of some 7000 to 10000 feet in length. As demand for air travel has grown so has the relative scarcity of this resource at many of the world's major airports. The construction of additional runways sufficiently close to major centres of population generally has not proved to be an acceptable proposition. Consequentially the allocation of take off and landing slots especially at at congested airports has been, and continues to be, of crucial concern to airline managers.

    The existing system used to allocate runway slots, has provided and continues to provide incumbent carriers with a highly effective means of preventing prospective operators from gaining access to their markets. It has proved to be a highly resilient barrier to market entry, although by no means the only way by which airlines have sought to exclude potential rivals. The system, organised under the auspices of the International Air Transport Association (IATA), involves the bringing together of some 500 delegates, representing 200 carriers, and between 80 and 90 airport scheduling coordinators at biannually held conferences. At these sessions an attempt is made to reach agreement on the allocation of slots at each major airport. The vast majority of people involved at these meetings are airline employees, as the latter group usually consists of staff of the major flag carriers. At Heathrow, for example, it is an employee of British Airways who as the airport scheduling coordinator works on a full-time independent basis organising the activities of the airport's scheduling committee and chairing its meetings.

    Historical precedence forms the main criterion in this apportioning process, hence the name 'grandfather rights' by which the system is generally referred. The result of this procedure is that those carriers currently operating the most flights to a given airport are able to exert a considerable degree of influence over the allocation of slots at that location. Companies with only a small number of rotations have substantially less ability to affect the final distribution. A great deal of horse trading ensues between the various operators, but newcomers having nothing to trade are forced to accept what is left, if anything.

3. Air France acquired a controlling interest in UTA in 1990. UTA's independent operations ceased at the end of 1992.

8 Devising a pro-competitive regulatory strategy for Europe's airlines

'Merger policy will have to play an important role in EC air transport. It is however unlikely to be able to deal with those fundamental characteristics of the airline industry which create the opportunity for anti-competitive behaviour in the first place, or with the extension of dominance which results from means other than merger or acquisition. This is so, even if the industry is prevented from becoming yet more concentrated.'

UK Civil Aviation Authority[1]

That companies ordinarily engage in activities aimed at enhancing their relative competitive positions is clear. However, because sometimes the competitive advantage created by the more successful of these tactics is so great as to eliminate existing competitors, dissuade potential rivals from entering a market, or force existing firms to operate in a manner that poses no competitive threat to the instigator, they are often regarded by governments as being unacceptable. It is a matter of political judgement as to which of these multifarious practices is consistent with the best interests of society. Given the inherently subjective nature of such decision making, it would seem sensible that right from the outset a government should make clear to participants the exact rules of the game. Devising a sufficiently precise set of guidelines though to encompass all possible future eventualities is simply not a feasible proposition. Differences in political philosophy and perspective also mean that a universally acceptable formula cannot exist.

Nonetheless, it must rest with government to determine what should constitute an acceptable framework of behaviour. Increasingly in recent years, economic regulation has been regarded as too blunt and intrusive an instrument of public policy; one that has been ineffective and often counter-productive, acting against the best interests of consumers. Hence the attraction for removing all such controls. One important consequence of this has been that the balance of power has shifted in favour of established firms, for they have been provided with a stronger voice in the debate as to how much and in what precise ways they are to be constrained. Massaging public opinion and extending largesse to those with influence has become a major industry.

It would seem desirable that those charged with economic regulation retain sufficient power to prevent powerful airline consortia exploiting their customers. Prohibiting Europe's larger incumbent carriers from merging provides an important structural control mechanism. Given however increasing competition from US megacarriers and a number of rapidly growing low cost Far Eastern airlines, considerable pressure is likely to be exerted on regulators and their governments by carriers seeking to merge. The view recently expressed by the Chairman of Air France that in order not to disadvantage Europe's carriers the European Commission should not seek to prevent such activity, provides a good example of this.[2]

Even if large scale mergers are prevented however, it would be naive to assume that airlines will be willing to simply give up at this juncture and accept the status quo. Invariably, alternative means will be sought to achieve their objectives. Given this likelihood, it is apparent that considerable reliance will need to be placed by regulatory authorities on the use of antitrust legislation. It is far from clear though that this will pose sufficient of an obstacle to powerful carriers. Fine tuning such legislation into a set of workable guidelines can be expected to take many years and cost a great deal of time, effort and money. Additionally, within Europe the pursuance of strongly held national interests can be expected to further delay the implementation of an effective antitrust policy. The time factor is of particular critical importance here as delay will considerably advantage the larger carriers. As already has been apparent in many countries, most new entrants simply do not possess the financial stamina to sustain long campaigns against powerful incumbents.

One way out of this dilemma would appear to be offered by the prospect of franchising route licences. Most existing regulatory controls originally were adopted to protect the interests of flag carriers. In certain instances, however, they have been successfully adapted to introduce competition into city-pairs hitherto devoid of rivalry. The UK's Civil Aviation Authority has provided a number of good examples in this regard. Rather than going to the extreme of abandoning all existing economic controls, why not amend policy and reorientate it towards promoting a more competitive marketplace. As the US experience clearly showed, the greatest impact came from smaller new entrant carriers. Their ability to survive against larger and better endowed incumbents was, to say the least, poor. Europe's large incumbent carriers have the benefit of hindsight and know which tactics provide the best means of neutralising new entrants. As a consequence, life will be even tougher for newcomers this side of the Atlantic.

A franchising system would force carriers to compete periodically for route licences. It would also provide the regulatory authority with a greater element of control in the event of unforeseen anti-competitive tactics manifesting themselves. Forecasting the future with any degree of precision will always remain a forlorn hope. Whilst it is mostly the case that regulators are placed in the position of only being able to act after the event, a franchising approach does offer the prospect of enabling a greater degree of influence to be exerted ex-ante. For example, only the tenders of carriers who previously had been adjudged not to have acted in a collusive or anti-competitive manner could be considered when allocating a route franchise.

Such an approach it is argued below has the potential to offer a more effective, more reliable and less costly means of controlling anti-competitive behaviour.

8.1 Defining the Task

In order to undertake such an evaluation it would seem appropriate first of all to define which objective(s) most governments have been keen to pursue. Of key concern it would appear has been the desire to create a sustainable competitive environment. This as the UK's Civil Aviation Authority has argued provides ...'...the best available mechanism to ensure the widest possible range of choices for users, that service quality is maintained and that fares are set at reasonable levels in relation to cost, as well as ... a powerful incentive to efficient operation and the sound allocation of resources'.[3] It follows from this hypothesis that anything that acts in such a way as to restrict competition is likely to have a detrimental impact on the achievement of one or all of these goals. The number of competitors necessary to produce a satisfactory standard with regard to these factors however cannot be determined scientifically. It is perfectly feasible that such a requirement could be satisfied by the presence of just two carriers on a route, but it is also possible that a similar route served by as many as four companies would not produce the desired outcome. All depends on the nature of the commercial relationships existing between the various participants.

One standard technique often used when undertaking an evaluation of this nature involves the selection of a number of near identical city-pair markets such that the two approaches could be tested simultaneously. If one adopts the UK CAA's stated objectives as being typical of most regulatory authorities, it would follow that three factors should form the prime focus of attention in such a comparison, namely: unit cost, yield and level of service.[4] In practice, such an exercise would be extremely difficult to undertake, not only because routes with near identical economic characteristics would be hard to find, but also because it would be unlikely that regulatory authorities would be willing to undertake the necessary experimentation.[5] In addition, and of crucial importance, a clear result could not be expected to emerge for a number of years. Given the real danger that the intervening period would be used by larger incumbent carriers to develop ever more control over their markets, it is imperative that an answer to the question as how best to ensure an on-going competitive environment is forthcoming as soon as is possible. This need for urgency necessitates the adoption of an alternative approach. Reliance on a comparative assessment of the two schemes anticipated merits, partly based on relevant past experience, offers such an alternative. True, it is a far from scientific approach to the matter, but in the anticipated circumstances provides the only viable means by which to proceed.

8.2 Controlling Competitive Behaviour

The method of approach adopted in this comparative assessment involves firstly identifying the more successful competition limiting strategies pursued by US carriers, secondly outlining the particular mechanisms that the antitrust and franchising approaches would employ to curtail each of these activities, thirdly providing a subjective judgement as to which is likely to prove more effective in each instance, and finally producing an overall summary of the main advantages and disadvantages of the two alternatives.

Table 8.1 lists the various forms of competitive device that have been exploited by US airlines over the past decade.[6] The regulatory mechanism for dealing with each activity is identified for both the antitrust and franchising approaches. For the purpose of this exercise the problem is explored within a European context.

Table 8.1   Methods to Control Competition Limiting Behaviour

Activity	Mechanism	
	Anti-Trust	**Franchising**
Hub Dominance	Anti-Merger	Carrier selection
Excess Capacity	Limit capacity	Revoke franchise
Predatory Pricing	Limit fares	Revoke franchise
Agency Commission	Impose standards	Stipulated in franchise
CRS exploitation	Impose standards	Impose standards

Activity	Mechanism	
	Anti-Trust	**Franchising**
Frequent Flyer	Ban activity	Ban activity
Slot control	Impose standards	Stipulated in franchise
Gate control	Impose standards	Stipulated in franchise
Collusion	Ban activity	Carrier selection

i) Hub Dominance

This is already a significant feature of Europe's scheduled airline markets. The European Commission is seeking to prevent this situation from worsening through the use of anti-merger controls. How effective this will be in practice remains to be seen, but even if it does succeed in preventing a number of powerful carriers from merging it is not at all obvious that some form of collusive activity will not immediately follow. Under antitrust, it will take many years to develop a sufficiently precise and workable set of guidelines where collusion is concerned. By the time an acceptable means of controlling the activity has evolved it may well prove too late. For by then sufficient time will have elapsed for the larger carriers to have eliminated their weaker rivals. In many respects, it is the long period of time that it is likely to take the Commission to implement an effective set of antitrust rules that forms one of the strongest arguments in favour of a franchising approach. Under such a system, hub dominance could be tackled directly, through the initial choice of carrier. One criterion in the awarding of a franchise being the likelihood of this activity occurring.

ii) Excess Capacity

The use of excess capacity provision would be handled under antitrust by the regulator stipulating the number of seats that the offending airline could offer on the particular route, after such behaviour had become apparent. Under a franchising system, action of this nature would invite revocation of the franchise and could therefore be anticipated to provide a stronger deterrent.

iii) Predatory Pricing

Under both antitrust and franchising systems it would be necessary for the regulating authority to investigate each and every case of such alleged action to determine that the aim had been to stifle competition. The advantage of franchising

127

is that the regulator would retain the power to force the offending carrier off the route in question, either immediately, or at the next tendering round. Forcing carriers to compete periodically for route licences would provide the regulator with an additional powerful control mechanism not available under antitrust.

iv) Travel Agency Commissions

The use of large commissions to influence travel agents to book their clients on the services of a particular airline would again need to be proven conclusively to be aimed at eliminating competition under both approaches. As in the case of predatory pricing, under franchising unfair action of this kind could be curtailed through loss of the route licence.

v) CRS Exploitation

Exploitation of the CRS has proved to be of such significance in the US that it has already provoked the setting of standards in Europe with regard to their use. Given the satisfactory implementation of these guidelines it is anticipated that further measures would be unnecessary.

vi) Frequent Flyer Programmes

As regards the use of frequent flyer programmes it is anticipated that under both antitrust and franchising the practice would be outlawed, the taxing of beneficiaries being seen as both complex and controversial.

vii) Slot Controls

It is anticipated that a number of runway slots would be allocated with each franchise in order to prevent exploitation of this most scarce resource. With antitrust it will be necessary to develop a set of standards regarding their use. Already this is proving to be a highly controversial matter and could ultimately involve legal action.

viii) Gate Availability

Gate availability could be expected to be handled in a similar manner to runway slots.

ix) Collusion

Under a franchising system the initial choice of carrier would form a crucial part in the fight against competition limiting behaviour. The aim would be to select a carrier that had formed no previous alliance or feeder arrangement with existing operators of the route, or group of routes, being tendered for franchise. Genuine rivalry would be the goal. To avoid excessive disruption to service provision and allow the regulatory authority to reduce the risk of strategic action by a consortium of carriers, the franchises available on each particular route would not come up for renewal at the same time. They would be spaced at regular intervals.

The penalties for anti-competitive activities are likely to be perceived by carriers as being more severe under franchising, given the possible loss of a route licence. The more likely course of action with the alternative approach would be for the offending carrier to be forced to curtail the particular activity and possibly face a fine. It is not at all obvious that this would prove sufficient of a deterrent to dissuade powerful and resourceful carriers from embarking on such a strategy.

Table 8.2 provides a general summary of the main advantages and disadvantages of the antitrust and franchising approaches.

Table 8.2   **Comparison of the Two Approaches**

Advantages of Antitrust

a) Greater freedom of choice for airlines, enabling them to take full advantage of available economies of scope, scale and density.

b) Less direct market intervention by the regulator - therefore potentially less costly and politically contentious.

Disadvantages of Antitrust

a) Need to determine in each case whether the particular activity is contravening regulations.

b) Delay in setting up a workable set of antitrust laws may be sufficient to allow powerful carriers to achieve positions of dominance that are irreversible.

c) Operates in an ex-post manner - action to curtail anti-competitive behaviour can only be undertaken after it has been apparent.

Advantages of Franchising

a) Provides a greater control over a developing competition limiting strategy.

b) Legal battles over what constitutes anti-competitive behaviour considerably reduced, as greater control retained by the regulator.

c) Provides for direct control of slots.

d) Growth of infrastructure can be taken into consideration in licence allocation.

Disadvantages of Franchising

a) Need to determine in each case whether the particular activity is contravening regulations.

b) Requires a ready availability of non-colluding rivals.

c) Maximum potential improvements in airline efficiency unlikely to be achieved, particularly in terms of economies of scope and density.

8.3 Ensuring a Sufficiently Competitive Environment

The licensing of additional carriers between specific airports with an accompanying allocation of slots and access to terminal facilities has the effect of introducing direct competition to existing city-pair markets. However, under present arrangements whenever such a policy has been adopted there has been a tacit understanding that the new services are to be additional to those already provided by existing operators. The protectionism inherent in the bilateral system has enabled incumbents to maintain their frequencies and dominant positions. Only in comparatively rare instances has direct head to head competition at comparable capacity levels been sanctioned. In the main, newcomers have been licensed only to operate from secondary airports. Invariably they have had little choice but to fit in with the existing collusive arrangement. The level of entry sanctioned usually has not been of a sufficient extent to enable a more radical approach by the new carrier to be at all viable. Once 'on board', the newcomer's best interest has been served by maintaining the status quo and discouraging any further entry. As a result, the competitive environment has not undergone any significant change, merely a minor redistribution of market share.

To achieve any substantial degree of entry to routes, particularly those involving congested airports and air space, requires that a certain amount of exiting also occurs. As the early stages of US deregulation clearly showed, new entrants with relatively small market shares can have a significant impact on overall behaviour. However, as has been aptly demonstrated, with economic freedom and given sufficient resources and effective managerial effort, such an irritation can be eliminated. Obtaining the desired efficiency gains and resulting lower fares without allowing powerful carriers a free hand to neutralise competitive pressures are perfectly feasible goals, providing some modification to existing regulatory policy is undertaken.

To prevent entry barriers being established, carriers should not be able to own or control airport facilities nor be the arbiters in allocating runway slots. Given the latter's tremendous scarcity, ultimate control for these should rest with the regulatory authority. Preventing airlines establishing powerful and long lasting impediments to competition of this kind is a vital requirement and would therefore need to form a central part of a revised and updated set of regulatory policies. Retaining the power to force carriers to exit routes on which they been able to manipulate market forces in furtherance of their own interests would appear to be crucial. For this, in reality, would appear to be the only way in which a regulatory authority can achieve the swift and decisive control essential to sustaining a strongly competitive marketplace. The adoption of a system of route franchising with carriers being forced periodically to compete for licences provides such a facility.

Notes

1. Submission of the Civil Aviation Authority to the House of Lords Committee dealing with the European Commission's Proposals for the Development of Civil Aviation in the Community, January 1990, p. 8.
2. Comments made by M. Bernard Attali at an aviation conference organised by the Financial Times in Singapore. Financial Times, 25 February 1992, p. 2.
3. Civil Aviation Authority, supra note 1, pp. 6-7.
4. The other matters identified by the CAA, namely of achieving as wide a choice for consumers and of providing an incentive for efficient resource allocation, do not lend themselves to any form of precise measurement. Given this, it would seem sensible to set them aside.
5. If one were to undertake such an exercise it would seem unreasonable to use the standards attained by charter carriers as suitable cost targets, given the different operating characteristics of their business. However, it would be reasonable to expect scheduled carriers to be able over a period of time to match the operating costs of the most efficient scheduled carrier. A former charter carrier that had moved into mainstream scheduled operations, such as Dan-Air, could provide such a set of suitable target levels.

   Fares would pose a more complex problem owing to the extent to which carriers rely on price discrimination. As a consequence of this, it would be necessary to set both average yield and full economy fare targets for each route type. New entrants would again be the most likely choice for a set of standards in this area.

As regards level of service, this would need to include not only in-flight quality, but also frequency and total seat availability.

In order to make this task more manageable the selection of a small number of general route types, each with their own specific economic characteristics, could be used to represent the full range of possibilities likely to be encountered in Europe. Using this yardstick approach, each particular market could then be set a reasonable target for the selected features. In this way, it would be possible to trace out the evolving competitive environment in each specific city-pair, so ensuring that competition was not being stultified. As in the case of telecommunications, the path towards selected target levels could be set in terms of an annual percentage reduction in costs and associated fares. Deviations from these norms could be expected to provoke investigation by the regulatory authority, which might ultimately result in market intervention. Such deviations could arise for a number of different reasons, but primarily they could be expected to result from the use of predatory behaviour and/or collusive action by larger and more powerful carriers.

6. The Commission lists as most significant the following predatory practices:

   a) provision of excess capacity on a route;

   b) setting fares appreciably below fully allocated costs;

   c) provision of override commissions to travel agents;

   d) use of frequent flyer programmes.

Explanatory Memorandum to the draft regulation providing for temporary relief against anti-competitive practices in the air transport sector, European Commission, 1990.

9 Implementing a franchising system

For the reasons discussed in the previous chapter, a franchising system is advocated. This is likely to prove much more robust in countering the competition constraining tactics of a powerful airline industry. Amending existing regulatory policy in such a way as to tackle directly the all important issue of market entry would appear to offer many advantages over the antitrust approach. Given its specific characteristics, the industry is naturally duopolistic. Under free market conditions, producers are able to acquire considerable market power and exploit it in both subtle and unsubtle ways to protect and enhance their markets. Acquiring the ability to control competition enables firms to be the arbiters in determining how much and in which particular markets to engage in such activities. The uncertainty of a competitive environment is virtually eliminated as a consequence. The US experience has shown how adept and imaginative airline managers can be in exploiting the specific features of their industry to achieve this. Few other industries have lent themselves to this degree of stage management.

The introduction of a franchising system would appear to offer a better prospect for achieving and preserving a competitive environment in the scheduled airline markets of Western Europe. Whilst it would be the case that maximum productive efficiency would be unlikely to result from the adoption of such a policy, given that all potential economies of scope and density would be unlikely to be exploited, the maintenance of competition would appear on balance to offer a better overall prospect for the consumer and overall economic welfare.[1]

Under such a regime, licences would come up for renewal and be tendered for every few years.[2] Only those routes or city-pairs which manifested the existence of powerful entry barriers would need to be incorporated within the franchising scheme. This would probably mean that virtually all of the existing major traffic routes within the twelve European Union Member States would require to be licensed. The number of franchises available for each route would be determined on the basis of existing traffic flows. As traffic levels increased, so could the number of carriers licensed to operate. Where a particular route did not appear to reflect normal traffic flows, special conditions would apply.[3] In certain instances, it may be that the award of franchises on the basis of groups of routes will be administratively more convenient both from the operators' and regulatory authority's viewpoints, and in addition be more satisfactory for users.

A small number of standard route types could be used as a basis for the purposes of comparison. Table 9.1 provides outline characteristics for three general types of city-pair market. Such a system would allow the appropriate regulatory body flexibility to amend the franchising terms governing individual routes in response to changing market conditions. In addition, in the unlikely event that an insufficient number of carriers bid for the available franchises, the authority could impose controls on fare levels and capacity if a monopoly were likely to result.

Table 9.1   Standard Route Types for Franchising Purposes

	Trunks	Secondary	Interregional
Range of traffic volumes (million pass. per year)	>1	>0.1	<0.1
Number of airlines	3 or 4	1 or 2	1
A/craft seating capacity	>150	<150	<100

As regards the type of entry barrier that would necessitate the incorporation of a route within the franchising system, the following would be of particular relevance:

i) insufficient take-off and landing slots;

ii) limitations in airport terminal facilities (including ownership or effective control of these by one or more carrier);

iii) domination of travel agencies in specific traffic generating locations by one or a small group of carriers' CRS.

In addition, once evidence of anti-competitive behaviour by one or more carrier on an unconstrained route manifested itself the route would become subject to franchise. This would tend to discourage the larger carriers from abusing their power.

9.1 Licence Allocation - The Tendering Process

In order to foster a competitive environment, all franchised routes would need to be subject to a tendering process every few years. In awarding franchises, regulatory authorities would need to take into consideration a number of factors, particularly:

i) the level and conditions (including availability) attached to each fare type that the airline had been offering on similar routes. New entrants would need to put forward specific estimates for the route in question;

ii) an approximate indication of the total amount of revenue the firm aimed to extract from its operations on the route;

iii) the total capacity the carrier planned to offer;

iv) the reliability of the company to date in fulfilling the conditions of previous franchise awards;

v) details of any interline arrangements or marketing agreements with connecting carriers, which were particularly relevant to the route;

vii) any restrictions on the distribution of tickets or exclusive deals with retailers.

In addition, special credit could be given for environmentally friendly and other generally beneficial proposals (e.g. the use of quiet/fuel efficient aircraft; the more efficient use of available infrastructure; and coordination with other transport modes).

Of crucial importance and the prime motive for proposing this particular approach however, is the desire to allow carriers considerable discretion in the ways in which they choose to operate. It would be their decision as to which route franchises they wished to tender for in the first place and it would be entirely up to them as to the precise ways in which they choose to operate them. Anti-competitive practices, as defined by the regulator, would be the one exception to this freedom of action. As the industry naturally lends itself to the successful exploitation of such activities, it falls to government to rule 'out of court' this unwelcome feature of economic freedom. Ensuring that carriers are forced periodically to compete for 'their' routes should act as a strong deterrent to airlines operating in this way, for, if discovered, they would have much to forfeit.

Providing that carriers had not colluded 'behind the scenes' in an attempt to carve up the total scheduled market and that for each route more airlines had tendered than the number of franchises available, it would fall upon the appropriate regulatory authority to make a judgement as to which company(s) to select. Evidence of any attempts to substantially limit competition would result in a carrier failing to renew its franchise. It is clear that those charged with regulating the industry would need to be especially vigilant in this matter. Ensuring the continuance of a healthy, but not excessively, competitive environment would be of key concern to the authority in determining which company(s) to award a franchise. A number of examples are given below to illustrate the approach that would need to be followed.

Case A

London(Heathrow) - Paris(CDG). Until 1990 the route was operated by the two flag carriers. British Midland is currently the third operator on the route. It would seem unlikely that this slot constrained route could support a fourth airline, especially after completion of the Channel Tunnel. Under a franchising regime, each licence awarded for the route would carry with it an entitlement to a reasonable number of take-off and landing slots spread throughout the day. In this way no one carrier would be unfairly advantaged.

Let us assume that the following carriers had tendered for the three available franchises: Aer Lingus, Air France, Air Littoral, British Airways, British Midland and Britannia. Each could be anticipated to fulfil the basic necessary conditions in terms of their safety record, financial viability and operating experience. Previous evidence of collusion between any of the above named would mean that only one of those involved could be awarded a franchise. A carrier noted for a strongly competitive stance, such as Britannia, could well provide sufficient of a spur to fulfil requirements. The inclusion of an airline which had earned a majority of its revenue from charter operations could be expected to have the effect of exerting a downward pressure on operating costs.

It probably would be politically expedient during the early operation of this system to include at least one French and one British carrier.

Case B

Manchester - Frankfurt. Currently operated by British Airways and Lufthansa, with each carrier operating two flights per day with 100/110 seat aircraft. Total annual traffic is approximately 150,000 passengers. To introduce an element of competition on this secondary route it would seem essential to replace at least one of the present incumbents with a carrier that had not operated in collusion with the remaining party. For example, BA could be replaced by Jersey European or Loganair. If this tactic did not produce a favourable outcome then the threat of the addition of a third carrier could have the effect of persuading the franchise holders to avoid collusive activity. It would be unlikely though that more than two carriers could operate efficiently on this type of route.

Case C

Leeds - Brussels. At present operated twice daily by one carrier, Sabena, using 30 seat aircraft. It is most unlikely that this type of route would necessitate inclusion in the franchising system.

In the event of collusion or other forms of competition limiting behaviour manifesting themselves, it may prove necessary to terminate a franchise before the normal expiry date. The onus in any investigation into alleged such malpractices would be on the carrier to prove that it was not contravening the conditions agreed when it commenced operating the franchised route. There would appear to be no necessity to control fares as the threat of the loss of a franchise should provide sufficient of a disincentive for carriers to engage in charging excessive prices. Predatory pricing would serve little purpose as the enforced withdrawal of one carrier from a route would result in the franchise being offered to other carriers.

Initially the tendering system could be operated by individual governments on a reciprocal basis, but ideally these activities should form an important part of the duties of a central European Union Regulatory Authority. The bilateral arrangements existing between Member States and external countries could continue as at present with each State determining policy, but once a common multinational practice had been agreed the same form of franchising system could be instituted if the route(s) in question were subject to high entry barriers. To benefit carriers based within the twelve Member States route franchises ordinarily would be awarded only to such airlines.

Notes

1. Two important preconditions here would be that all airlines were in private ownership and that there were no state subsidies to the sector.
2. Five years would appear to be a reasonable time interval in this regard, as a carrier would have sufficient time to establish itself on a route and to have operated profitably.
3. For example, if a national or regional government determined that operations to remote or difficulty accessed locations were not to be considered as normal commercial ventures, a system of direct subsidy could be introduced. A tendering system would be equally applicable in this situation with the lowest subvention being the determining factor in terms of which carrier to select. It would be necessary however for the regulator to stipulate a target level of service and the fares to be charged.

10 The quest for efficient regulation

Staunch advocates of the power of market forces regard as anathema any form of government intervention, arguing with some justification that inefficiency will be the only outcome. For this viewpoint to be at all convincing presupposes the existence of market forces sufficiently powerful to prevent individual participants acquiring control of their commercial environments. Entrepreneurial activity however, is undertaken on the expectation that sufficient financial reward will be forthcoming to justify the effort. In general, the larger the anticipated return the greater the willingness to innovate. Too many firms surviving in the same product market could act to stifle innovative effort, too few could result in consumers being exploited.

In many respects economists are much to blame for the confusion that abounds regarding the competitive process. The neoclassical model of perfect competition has invariably been used as a benchmark by which to assess other types of market structure. Such a market is perfect in the sense that the firms are all broadly of a similar size and capability and that a 'level playing field' exists, but the word 'competition' is entirely misplaced as the scope for rivalrous behaviour is near non-existent if the conditions for a perfectly competitive market are fulfilled. The model is simply not capable of providing any insight into the ways in which firms actually compete.

That firms ordinarily engage in activities designed to protect their interests against existing and would-be rivals is an entirely logical response; to anticipate otherwise would reflect a profoundly naive comprehension of basic human behaviour. A fine line exists however between actions that generally can be regarded as being legitimate competitive responses and those that are anti-competitive. For example, activity aimed at bankrupting a rival cannot automatically be identified as being of the latter type. Only if such actions succeed in dissuading other firms from competing in the particular product market can the process of competition be deemed to have been constrained. It does not always follow that a firm being forced out of business is the result of the anti-competitive behaviour of its former rivals. Indeed such activity may well be demonstrating that the competition is working effectively.[1]

The parameters of 'the market place' have altered fundamentally over the past two decades. Companies are no longer constrained in terms of the range of products they traditionally have produced. The tremendous developments in the fields of communications and information processing has also freed them of national identity. Mobility of capital and the search for the best return has turned each product marketplace into a global one. Achieving the best return for shareholders usually means searching the world for the best opportunities. Given both the enhanced ability of large firms to acquire and divest core activities and the requirement that they must earn comparable rates of return with others of their kind, the traditional link between the number of firms supplying a particular product market and the degree of competition existing between them may well no longer apply.

As a consequence, the potential conflict between efficiency and equity has become more complex and much more difficult to resolve. Deriving a consensus on such a controversial matter as where and under what conditions to sacrifice efficiency in favour of greater equity is in most instances an impossible task. There can be no one ideal balance, it is a matter of personal and collective preference. Devising a regulatory regime which recognises this reality requires tremendous ingenuity, as such a system would require considerable flexibility, providing those charged with carrying out the task an ability to respond to the changing characteristics of individual markets and varying general political demands. The extremes of the political pendulum, so often reflecting changes in public policy in matters concerning economic regulation, would strongly militate against the likelihood of such an achievement.

Adequate information disclosure by those subject to economic control forms another stumbling block in the quest for efficient regulation. The need to keep abreast of all developments in the industry would necessitate a close monitoring by the appropriate authority. This would be both expensive to undertake and tend to counterbalance the attributed benefits of the policy.

In general, markets have become increasingly dynamic providing those responsible with regulating them with a tremendous challenge. Such rapidly changing conditions necessitates a flexible approach, any process that encourages entrenched attitudes to develop needs to be avoided at all costs. Ideally a regulatory authority should be in a position to accurately predict the strategic tactics and responses of firms and as a consequence be ready to counter any attempts to further constrain or expand competition beyond that which has been deemed to be in the public interest. Unforeseen developments, the result of technical innovation for example, make it essential that the regulator retains the ability to substantially alter the level and/or form of intervention. Policy ideally should evolve in a gradual and systematic way, avoiding wherever possible the abrupt volte-face associated with previous attempts at regulating industry.

Hopefully, a more balanced and realistic attitude to market intervention will eventually emerge, one that is both devoid of political bias and fundamentally recognises the manner by which firms seek to achieve their objectives. That efficient regulation is without doubt an unattainable pipe-dream, does not imply that such activities are not in themselves worthwhile. On the contrary, the globalisation of business more than ever requires that adequate safeguards be provided by governments to protect their citizens against modern day buccaneering.

Notes

1. For example, James Goldsmith perceives himself not as a corporate raider, but as a saviour of weary corporations. Sampson, A. (1989), The Midas Touch, Hodder & Stoughton, pp. 40-59.

11 Recent developments

11.1 The US Market

With the exception of Southwest, all major US carriers have experienced heavy financial losses during the early 1990s. Continuing over supply in the domestic market, partly the result of Chapter 11 bankruptcy protection and partly the outcome of economic recession, has resulted in fierce price competition. More recently, there have been indications that this precarious situation is drawing to a close, albeit until the next recession hits.

A good deal of financial restructuring has been undertaken in the interim, with only one major carrier now operating under Chapter 11. Continental and TWA emerged from this state in 1993, Air Canada playing a major role in enabling the former to rejoin the financially solvent by acquiring a 29% shareholding in the carrier. TWA, now considerably reduced in size, continues to be unattached, but this situation is unlikely to prevail for long. Table 11.1 provides a summary of the recent financial performances of the majors and their current status.

Aside from American, Delta and United with their extensive international route networks and the lean Southwest concentrating exclusively on domestic operations, other carriers have required financial input from airlines outside of the US to ensure their survival. Even the big three though are being forced to find radical new means by which to compete against the highly successful Southwest. The setting up of low cost subsidiaries able to match the latter's unit cost and productivity levels may prove to be their best hope. The alternative involves franchising out services to existing low cost operators, possibly utilising feeder airlines already contractually tied.

A small number of new entrants have appeared during the recent recession, most notably Kiwi and Reno Air. These carriers have taken advantage of the very low leasing rates for aircraft and an over supplied labour market. Whether these small companies remain other than a minor irritant remains to be seen, but a repetition of the Southwest experience from this source would appear most unlikely.

Table 11.1   **Recent Financial Results of US Majors**

Carrier	Net Figure ($m)			Status
	1991	**1992**	**1993**	
American	-165	-735	-110	
America West	-222	-132	37	Operating under Chapter 11 protection
Continental	-341	-299	- 39*	29% shareholding by Air Canada
Delta	-239	-565	-226	
Northwest	- 3	-386	-115	20% shareholding by KLM
Southwest	27	91	170	Domestic carrier
TWA	35	-318	-450	
United	-335	-933	- 50	
USAir	-260	-1228	-393	25% shareholding by British Airways

(* last 8 months)

Source: Air Transport World, June 1993, p. 63 - 4; & March 1994, p. 12.

11.2 Europe - Continuing Liberalisation

The Commission's third package of liberalising measures became effective in January 1993. Whilst implementation of the package represented a major further step in the removal of economic regulations, a number of thorny issues, particularly state aid and slot allocation, were passed over to be tackled separately at a later date. Political reality precluded a more encompassing development. A summary of the measures currently in force is contained in table 11.2. As is evident, unconstrained cabotage does not become a reality until 1997.

The continuing gradual removal of economic controls has not produced any dramatic changes. There has been neither a general lowering of fares nor a rapid influx of airlines onto routes previously the preserve of the associated flag carriers.

Airlines in the main have proceeded cautiously, their responses conditioned partly by the deep economic recession that has afflicted much of Europe during the 1990s and partly by the poor experience of carriers whose more opportunistic and adventurous tactics have proved with hindsight to have been little more than ill considered folly. It is apparent that the mavericks have lacked the clear and sound judgement essential for survival in this highly cyclical of industries.

By comparison, the methodical, systematic and gradual approach, as exemplified by British Midland for example, has proven to be the hallmark of success. When competition emanates from a stable and shrewd source, as with this carrier, the benefits to the travelling public are likely to prove much more durable. All full fare passengers now travelling between London (Heathrow) and Paris (Charles de Gaulle) have benefited from the introduction of services on to the route by British Midland. The return fare charged by Air France and British Airways in autumn 1992 of £316 was undercut by the market entrant by £60. By the summer of 1993, all three carriers were charging £240. Gains to air travellers of this nature, as the CAA[1] has commented, remain the exception however, being confined to routes on which carriers such as the above mentioned have been able to muster sufficient airport slots to commence a satisfactory level of service.

Table 11.2   Measures Agreed by the Council of Ministers in 1992

Right of Establishment

Common standards set for the granting and maintenance of air carrier operating licences, effective from 1994. These include standards dealing with financial fitness and technical issues involving aircraft use. In addition, the majority ownership of a licensed carrier must be within the Union. (Exemptions were granted to Britannia, Monarch and SAS on this latter issue.)

Market Access

Full fifth and seventh[2] freedom rights effective from January 1993, but unrestricted cabotage delayed until April 1997.

Domestic routes to remain subject to the control of individual member states until 1997, but discrimination on the grounds of carrier ownership or national identity is prohibited.

Monopoly rights on domestic routes to be allowed until 1996, if alternative transport services are not available.

Public service obligations may be imposed by Member States to maintain scheduled services to economically developing or deprived regions. Three year exclusive rights may be granted in such instances, but these are subject to a Union wide tendering process.

Air traffic distribution systems of individual Member States continue to apply, including those determined by congestion and matters of an environmental nature.

Capacity

New inter-regional services operated by aircraft with an 80 seat maximum capacity or with fewer than 30,000 seats provided annually may be protected by Member States from competition involving the use of larger equipment.

If serious financial damage is likely to be inflicted on a Union registered scheduled carrier, whilst capacity controls are not permitted certain (unspecified) 'stabilising' measures may be sanctioned by the Commission.

Fares

Full pricing freedom covering both scheduled and charter sectors. The only routes exempt are those on which a public service obligation applies.

Individual Member States and the Commission may intervene:

i) in the event of fully flexible fares being excessive in relation to long term costs;

ii) when very low fares result in heavy losses; and

iii) if predatory pricing is suspected.

Source: T. French (1992), 'The European Commission's Third Air Transport Liberalisation Package', EIU Travel & Tourism Analyst, No. 5.

An essential characteristic differentiating Europe's flag carriers concerns their ownership. Whilst private sector companies have been pruning and honing their operating practices for many years in anticipation of greater competition, the same has not been true of their state-owned counterparts. As a consequence, this latter group have faced considerable financial difficulties as their previously secure markets have been opened up to competitors. In the past when faced with such a predicament the owning state could have been relied upon to make good the loss. Life is no longer quite so simple however, as the European Commission now requires that state aid be used only for the purposes of restructuring. Whilst not a subject of the third package of liberalising measures, the Commission is determined that this process of bailing out Europe's least efficient carriers should not continue. Aid packages are being subject to ever greater scrutiny, with increasingly tight conditions being placed on the recipient.

Attempts by Europe's state-owned airlines to bring down their operating cost levels to match those of privatised carriers such as British Airways and KLM, are proving exceedingly difficult. Size has not proved to be a significant factor in this regard, with all of the state-owned airlines requiring to be restructured. Aer Lingus, Air France, Iberia, Olympic and TAP have each required aid on at least one occasion from their respective governments to enable them to remain financially afloat whilst undertaking at least some of the necessary cost-cutting measures essential for their survival. The painful transition from state-owned utility to commercial enterprise has hit hardest the flag carriers of those countries that previously had adopted the most conservative stance towards liberalisation. For example, in 1993 the chairman of Air France was forced out of office as a result of pressure on the French Government by the carrier's workforce, who were objecting to enforced redundancies. As yet, no European flag carrier has been allowed by its government to succumb to financial pressures. Given that measures to ease the financial burden of flag carriers can take many guises[3], their elimination will be far from easy. Political reality makes it unlikely that state aid will be eliminated either easily or swiftly from Europe's airline industry.

11.3 Reactions of European Carriers

On a positive note, there has been some response from carriers to the route access opportunities available to them since the beginning of 1993. In the majority of cases airlines have been taking advantage of fifth and seventh freedom rights, but there have been a few instances of sixth and eighth freedoms being exercised.[4] By March 1994 some 35 examples of 'new' routes being operated were apparent, the details of which are contained in table 11.3.

Table 11.3   Route Opportunities arising from the Third Package

Freedom	Routing	Carrier
Fifth	(Lyon) - Toulouse - Madrid - Lisbon	Air France
	(Milan) - Brussels - Dublin	Alitalia
	(Milan) - Frankfurt - Oslo	Alitalia
	(London) - Turin - Thessaloniki	British A/w
	(Helsinki) - Gothenburg - Amsterdam	Finnair*
	(Helsinki) - Dusseldorf - Barcelona	Finnair*
	(Madrid) - Amsterdam - Stockholm	Iberia
	(Barcelona) - Amsterdam - Copenhagen	Iberia

Freedom	Routing	Carrier
Fifth	(Reykjavik) - Stockholm - Oslo	Icelandair*
	(Reykjavik) - Copenhagen - Hamburg	Icelandair*
	(Amsterdam) - Luxembourg - Strasburg	KLM
	(Amsterdam) - Gothenburg - Helsinki	KLM
	(Copenhagen) - Brussels - Lyon	SAS
	(Lisbon) - Copenhagen - Stockholm	TAP
Sixth	Hamburg - (Milan) - Barcelona	Alitalia
	Oslo - (London) - Athens	British A/w
	Copenhagen - (London) - Malaga	British A/w
	Stavanger - (London) - Paris	British A/w
	Dublin - (London) - Antwerp	British A/w#
Seventh	Paris - Copenhagen	British A/w@
	Paris - Munich	British A/w@
	Paris - Stockholm	British A/w@
	Berlin - Oslo	British A/w$
	Berlin - Stockholm	British A/w$
	Dresden - Paris	British A/w$
	Stuttgart - Lyon	British A/w$
	Stuttgart - Nice	British A/w$
	Stuttgart - Venice	British A/w$
	Barcelona - Venice	Sabena
Eighth	(Rome) - Barcelona - Valencia	Alitalia
	(Milan) - Barcelona - Malaga	Alitalia
	(London) - Hanover - Leipzig	British A/w
	(Amsterdam) - Lisbon - Porto	KLM
	(Copenhagen) - Barcelona - Madrid	SAS
	(Antwerp) - London - Liverpool	VLM

(* Permitted under the second package until July 1994; # operated by Cityflyer Express; @ operated by TAT; $ operated by Deutsche BA.)

Source: S. Guild, Airline Business, March 1994, p. 45.

Whilst the above clearly does not represent a massive response to the opportunities available under the third package, the economic recession currently afflicting much of Europe undoubtedly has been instrumental in producing this muted outcome. Nonetheless, it is apparent that carriers are actively engaged in the task of identifying routes that are likely to prove sensible targets for entry. Opportunities may arise for many reasons. For example, it may well be that the existing operator of a prospective route is perceived in a bad light by travellers because of general unreliability, poor frequency of service, high fares, low quality in-flight service, or possibly all four. If, in addition, the carrier in question experiences high operating costs, the prospect of an entrant being able to provide a better quality of service whilst simultaneously undercutting existing fares would be high. It would appear from the above table that certain routes involving Barcelona have been identified by a number of carriers as fitting this description.

Another instance involves situations in which passengers currently flying between two locations are required to change airline or aircraft en route. The provision of a through service not involving a change of aircraft is likely to prove more attractive, increasing load factors on services that previously had been marketed separately. The sixth freedom rights exercised by British Airways involving flights routed via Gatwick, provide a good example of this opportunity being exercised.

The Belgian carrier VLM provides yet another example of opportunism, it being the first airline to exercise cabotage in the UK market. By extending its Antwerp to London (City Airport) service to Liverpool, the carrier has reactivated a UK domestic route that previously had been operated by British Midland to Heathrow. The latter had abandoned the route in 1991 to make better use of its slots at the capital's congested airport.

Most obvious though of the opportunities recently provided is the enhanced ability to access feeder traffic for long haul services. This is very much of a two edged sword however, for all carriers have much to gain from this particular practice.

11.4 Alliance Activity of European Carriers

Against the background of gradual liberalisation, Europe's scheduled carriers have been engaged in a number of activities aimed at securing their survival in an increasingly global marketplace. Of Europe's three largest airlines, British Airways is widely recognised as being the most successful, as is evident from the financial results detailed in table 11.4. The company has been at the forefront of alliance development activity, its particular approach involving the part acquisition of its partners. To gain access to the domestic US market, in January 1993 the carrier acquired a 25% shareholding in USAir. It followed this two months later by buying a similar stake in Qantas. Within Europe the airline has sought to gain direct access to two of the continent's main traffic generating areas by taking over locally based carriers. In France the company purchased 49% of the equity of TAT European A/l and in Germany a similar level of shareholding was acquired in regional carrier Delta Air (since renamed Deutsche BA). Whilst these latter two purchases provide it with a much greater degree of control than would be available under a looser arrangement with independent carriers, the outcome to date cannot be said to have been entirely satisfactory. Losses at TAT for example, have been heavy. When taken in conjunction with the very poor financial performance of USAir, it is apparent that alliance building activity of this kind is not without its tribulations.

Table 11.4   Net Financial Results of European Flag Carriers ($m)

Carrier	1990	1991	1992	% State-Owned
Aer Lingus	8	- 18	-196	100
Air France	-132	- 12	-617	96
Alitalia	- 82	- 28	- 12	85
Austrian	52	11	0	52
British A/w	170	687	298	0
Finnair	- 19	- 13	- 17	70
Iberia	-138	-347	-340	100
KLM	-347	66	-319	38
Lufthansa	9	-258	-250	51
Luxair	n.a.	4	1	23
Olympic	-164	-134	-225	100
SAS	-145	-239	-127	50
Sabena	-206	- 69	12	25
Swissair	- 16	58	81	20
TAP	- 15	- 38	-200	100

Source: Airline Business, September 1993, pp. 78 - 81; & 'The Skies in 1993', Airline Business, p. 13, & pp. 64 - 65.

Europe's two other large carriers, Air France and Lufthansa, have both been forced to concentrate on reducing their comparatively high operating cost levels. In this regard Lufthansa has had considerably more success than its partner, expecting to break even in 1994. The two airlines formed an alliance partnership with each other in 1991 which did not involve any equity transfer, but there has been little apparent symbiosis. More recently, Lufthansa has concentrated on establishing an alliance with United, which has resulted in a number of code-sharing activities.

Whilst the big three have had some degree of choice in deciding their future courses of action, Europe's smaller carriers have had little option but to either join forces with a larger neighbour or merge with others of a similar kind. The latter course of action is much more difficult to realise however, as was demonstrated by the Alcazar project. Alcazar involved the merger of four airlines - Austrian, KLM, SAS and Swissair. The aim was to create a carrier large enough to compete on equal terms with the likes of Air France, British Airways and Lufthansa. A number of difficulties emerged with the proposal, a key factor highlighted at the time of abandonment being the choice of US alliance partner. Prior to the merger proposals KLM had acquired a major shareholding in Northwest, SAS was similarly involved with Continental and Swissair had a 5% cross-shareholding with Delta. It only really made commercial sense to have an alliance with one major US carrier, but strong ties existed between each of the three European airlines and their respective partners. In the event it proved an impossible choice to make. Another major issue, played down at the time, concerned the question of where the inevitable cuts in staffing levels would occur.

Before the Alcazar project was abandoned, Austrian had been made an alternative offer by Lufthansa, which had much to loose from the proposed merger. Whether or not the offer from Lufthansa was based on a genuine interest in Austrian or simply aimed at promoting disharmony between Alcazar's partners remains a matter of conjecture. Since the demise of the project, the three European Quality Alliance members, Austrian, SAS and Swissair, have sought to explore further collaborative possibilities with each other, whilst KLM has concentrated on developing its ties with Northwest.

The above represents the type of alliance building that catches public attention. Perhaps of even greater significance, but undoubtedly far less newsworthy, have been the multiplicity of code-sharing arrangements that airlines have made with each other. Whilst the larger airlines have able to attract sufficient traffic levels to maintain and expand their international networks using their own resources, smaller carriers have been faced with a stark choice on all but their densest routes and traditional links with their former colonies. The latter have had either to face the prospect of pulling out of many of their former destinations or find some means by which to share the burden. Given the undoubted unattractiveness of the former option, most have chosen to follow the latter course of action. By way of example, table 11.5 lists the long haul destinations served by Sabena in 1984 and 1993, and table 11.6 provides similar information for SAS. As is apparent, whilst the vast majority of destinations listed were served by the two airlines on their own accounts in 1984, both airlines have now either withdrawn from their non-core markets or are undertaking them in the form of joint code-sharing services with other carriers.[5]

Table 11.5 **Long Haul Destinations of Sabena**

Destination	Weekly Frequency 1984	Weekly Frequency 1993	Nature of 1993 Operation
Africa			
Abidjan	2	2	On own account
Bamako	1	2	On own account
Banjul	0	3	On own account
Brazzaville	1	1	On own account
Bujumbura	3	3	On own account
Conakry	2	4	On own account
Cotonou	0	2	On own account
Dakar	3	3	On own account
Dar-es-Salaam	1	0	Connection via Nairobi
Douala	1	1	On own account
Entebbe	1	3	On own account
Freetown	0	1	On own account
Johannesburg	3	2	On own account
Kano	1	1	On own account
Kigali	5	3	On own account
Kilimanjaro	1	0	
Kinshasa	5	2	On own account
Lagos	2	4	On own account
Libreville	1	1	On own account
Lome	0	2	On own account
Luanda	0	2	On own account
Monrovia	2	0	
Nairobi	2	3	On own account
Asia			
Bangkok	2	0	Air France connection via Paris
Bombay	1	0	Air France connection via Paris
Kuala Lumpur	2	0	
Manila	1	0	
Singapore	2	0	Air France connection via Paris
Tokyo	2	3	Joint service with All Nippon

Destination	Weekly Frequency		Nature of 1993 Operation
	1984	1993	
Middle East			
Abu Dhabi	1	0	
Dubai	2	0	
Jeddah	2	0	
North America			
Atlanta	3	7	Joint service operated by Delta
Boston	0	5	On own account
Chicago	3	4	On own account
Montreal	3	0	Air France connection via Paris
New York	7	7	On own account

Table 11.6   **Long Haul Destinations of SAS**

Destination	Weekly Frequency		Nature of 1993 Operation
	1984	1993	
Africa			
Dar-es-Salaam	2	0	Swissair connection via Zurich
Johannesburg	1	0	Austrian connection via Vienna
Nairobi	1	0	Swissair connection via Zurich
Asia			
Bangkok	3	7	
Beijing	0	4	
Calcutta	2	0	Connection via Bangkok
Hong Kong	0	3	
Karachi	2	0	Swissair connection via Zurich
Singapore	3	7	
Tokyo	4	7	
Middle East			
Jeddah	3	0	
North America			
Chicago	4	4	Joint service operated by Austrian
Los Angeles	4	5	
New York	8	11	
Seattle	4	3	
South America			
Montevideo	1	0	Connection via Rio de Janeiro

Destination	Weekly Frequency		Nature of 1993 Operation
	1984	1993	
Rio de Janeiro	2	3	Joint service operated by Varig
Santiago	1	0	Connection via Rio de Janeiro
Sao Paulo	2	3	Joint service operated by Varig

11.5 Global Alliance Activity

In the main carriers have sought to concentrate their activities in regions of the world over which they possess a comparative advantage. By focusing resources on their core markets, airlines have provided themselves with the best means of defence against rivals. This strategy alone is of itself not sufficient to ensure long term prosperity. Having access to the major airline markets of the world undoubtedly is of great importance. Over 72% of the total demand for air transport is accounted for by six geographically specific markets. These in order of importance are: Internal US (29.4%), Intra-Europe (13.4%), Transatlantic (10.9%), Intra-Asia (8.9%), Pacific (6.5%) and Europe-Asia (3.0%)[6]. To qualify as a global carrier necessitates a significant presence in each of these regions. How best this can be achieved remains the critical question.

Under ideal conditions one obvious solution for a powerful airline would be to acquire controlling interests in carriers holding similar positions to itself in other major world markets. If this were to occur, it would be perfectly feasible for nearly all of the world's airline services to be supplied by fewer than ten globally integrated megacarriers. Fortunately for consumers such ideal circumstances do not prevail. Aside from political factors, it would seem most unlikely that carriers from different areas of the world could be amalgamated in such a manner that the resulting organisation was both efficient and innovative. The sheer practical problem of fusing together a number of distinct commercial operations in such a manner as to produce a cohesive and effectively functioning single entity renders this outcome unrealistic.

In practice a number of strategies have been apparent. Of these, perhaps the closest to the ideal cited above has been that exemplified by British Airways. This has involved the carrier acquiring large minority shareholdings in its intended partners. Opportunities for this type of purchase usually have arisen for one of three reasons: either the potential carrier has faced dire financial difficulties and has had little option but to accept the prospect of losing its independence, or the airline in question has been in the process of being privatised, or the airline has become available as a result of regulatory intervention. In the case of the UK flag carrier, partners have been acquired via all three routes.

To acquire large minority shareholdings in prospective partners requires substantial amounts of capital. Very few carriers have been in the enviable position of British Airways of having sufficient finance available for this purpose. Perhaps if financial results had not been so bad in recent years, more carriers would have had the resources to engage in this type of activity. However, given the undoubted difficulties that acquiring carriers have faced in turning their new charges into profitable assets, maybe even given available capital this would not have occurred.

Another approach involving equity transfer rests on the interested parties acquiring small cross-shareholdings in each other. Mutual recognition of the strength and standing of each partner forms the basis of this arrangement, as is shown by the Delta, Singapore Airlines and Swissair alignment. Table 11.7 provides a summary of alliance activity which has involved acquisition.

Table 11.7   **Global Alliance by Acquisition**

Europe	USA	S. America	Far East	Australasia

British A/w------USAir(25%)---Qantas(25%)

Iberia-----------------------------------Aerolineas Argentinas(85%)
                                                              Ladeco(37%)
                                                              Viasa(40%)

KLM--------------Northwest(20%)

Swissair(5%)----Delta(5%)-----------------------------Singapore(5%)

Given limited financial resources, most carriers have had to seek less costly means by which to expand (and in some cases maintain) their route networks. Invariably this has involved airlines undertaking searches to find compatible partners. To ensure the success of a prospective alliance, it is essential that each of the parties involved each perceive that they are gaining from the arrangement. If not, it is likely that at some point one of the partners will conclude that its best interests are not being served and it will withdraw seeking to establish a more attractive alliance with a new partner. A number of instances of this occurring have been apparent over the past few years. Changes in market conditions which have nothing to do with the existing alliance partners, may also produce such an outcome.

Alliances usually involve some form of code-sharing, in which the carriers involved each indicate that a specific flight being operated is their own. For example, Sabena and Delta's joint service from Brussels to Atlanta is advertised as SN125 by Sabena and DL125 by Delta. In some arrangements, as in this particular case, one of the partners operates all the flights. The exact nature of the commercial agreement between the participants varies, not all being based on a sharing of costs and a pooling of revenues. One variant involves the carrier not operating the particular service agreeing to purchase a certain proportion of the available capacity at an agreed rate. What is clear is that a multiplicity of deals are now in existence and that the process of finding the ideal partner in order to establish the best possible code-sharing deal is very much a dynamic on-going process.

11.6 Overview

The consensus of opinion amongst most airline industry experts is that if left entirely to market forces no more than ten consortia would survive the restructuring process triggered by deregulation. Rather unexpectedly, it is the area of revenue generation, rather than cost, that is thought to have produced this outcome.

Whilst governments of the world have professed a general commitment to allowing unfettered competition to occur in the sector, several have demonstrated an unwillingness to accept the full destructive aspects of the process. For example, the avowed belief of successive US governments in the superiority of market forces appears curiously compromised by bankruptcy protection legislation that in effect has rewarded weak carriers by providing them with what many have regarded as an unfair advantage over their victors (in name only). Requests to the European Commission by a number of governments to allow further injections of state aid to enable their high cost flag carriers to undertake essential restructuring in order for them to match their more efficient rivals form another example of this lack of conviction. Given these occurrences, it is difficult not to conclude that, despite the rhetoric, very few governments in practice possess either the political stomach to accept the full rigours of market forces, or have sufficient belief that deregulation will produce an enduring competitive environment.

Undoubtedly airline users have benefited as a result of competition. There have even been reductions in full economy/business fares on certain intra-European routes, one of the last bastions of the old protectionist regime. Given the airline industry as it currently exists and the comments made above, it would appear unlikely that more than a total of three (or four) globally integrated and organised carriers will emerge. The industry is also likely to feature a wide array of code-sharing agreements between more loosely aligned partners. Whilst the overall impact will be to increase supplier concentration, many observers would argue that it is still too early to judge whether this will result in less competition.

Notes

1. Airline Competition in the European Single Market, Civil Aviation Authority.
2. The seventh freedom of the air enables a carrier registered in country A to operate a service between countries B and C independently of its own services from A to B and C.
3. State aid has manifested itself in many forms ranging from reduced landing fees and aircraft handling charges, low interest loans, training grants, to direct subvention.
4. The sixth freedom of the air enables a carrier registered in country B to carry passengers and freight from country A to country C on through services operated via B. The eighth freedom of the air relates to the right of cabotage.
5. Whilst SAS has pulled out of operating its own services to many of its former long haul destinations, it has initiated operations to a small number of new locations in the Far East. By contrast, Sabena has concentrated on expanding its network of routes to Africa.
6. Coombs, T. (1993), 'Surviving the new world order', Avmark Aviation Economist, April.

Conclusion

US deregulation has had a profound impact on the strategic development of airlines all over the world. The economics of operating scheduled airline services has been transformed as a consequence of economic freedom. The lessons gleaned from the US experience, particularly those concerning the most effective ways of constraining rivals, have been quickly adopted by carriers facing the opening up to competition of their own local markets. In addition, in response to the hunt by the successful US survivors for further international traffic, carriers have been forced to emulate certain of the tactics adopted by these megacarriers, virtually irrespective of their own government's regulatory stance.

In contrast to the US, Canada and Australia, the approach in Europe has been one of slow and gradual liberalisation, partly the result of the wide range of view apparent amongst the twelve nation States that comprise the European Union. Despite the apparent common view, individual national vested interests continue to form the primary driving force within this supranational organisation. Given this reality, it is difficult to envisage one of the more powerful Member States allowing its major carrier to be adversely affected by Union policy. Even with a share of peak time runway slots the likelihood of small independent carriers surviving to operate scheduled airline services is remote. As evidenced by the US experience, the ability of large incumbent carriers to contain the destructive elements of the competitive process, not only through the control of takeoff and landing slots, is prodigious. The eventual outcome in Europe, despite the best efforts of the Commission, will replicate the experience of other deregulated airline markets. The economics of the industry, particularly concerning revenue generation, leads one inexorably to such a conclusion.

This does not necessarily imply that, given such an outcome, competition would be minimal, all would depend on the aspirations of the surviving globally integrated megacarrier consortia. The likelihood though is that these powerful groups will conclude that in certain (perhaps the majority) of their markets it would not be in their individual interests to compete. In such circumstances it would be difficult to to establish conclusively that such behaviour was collusive. Reliance by regulatory authorities on anti-trust legislation to prevent competition being constrained in this manner would likely prove to be of only limited success. Ensuring that the competitive process cannot be artificially constrained by powerful suppliers irrespective of the manner in which they are aligned may well necessitate more direct forms of intervention. As is discussed in chapter nine, a system of franchising route licences offers one means by which to increase competitive pressure if it is adjudged that consumers are being exploited.

As regards other regions of the world, it is clear that faced with mounting financial difficulties many of South America's governments have been forced to privatise their national airlines. A major outcome of this policy has been that Iberia has acquired substantial shareholdings in no fewer than three South American flag carriers, Aerolineas Argentinas (85%), Ladeco (37%) and Viasa (45%). Spain's strong trading links with the continent, based on its former colonial ties, provides the motive for this strategy. Interestingly, this trend has not been observed in Africa; the comparative political instability of many African states and their low levels of economic activity being the main reasons. Financially weaker countries have faced formidable difficulties maintaining their flag carriers. Over the years several attempts have been made by neighbouring countries to jointly operate their scheduled air services, but most have ended in failure. The diverse economic and cultural interests of the various participants are likely to continue to render such collaborative ventures unviable. Africa's economically weaker nations face increasing dependence on the region's stronger carriers for the provision of their scheduled services.

The area of the world to look for future developments both in this sector and no doubt in many others, is the Far East. The low cost advantage of carriers based in the region, coupled with their deservedly high reputations for quality of in-flight service, has made them formidable opponents. The high economic growth rates of the region seem certain to continue, the balance of world economic power shifting further away from the West as a consequence. Carriers based in the Far East will benefit the most from this transformation. Given the greater incorporation into the world economy of China, the Far East's most populous country, it is not difficult to imagine the key to longer term development resting somewhat ironically with this most ancient of cultures. Further speculation is certainly justified.

There can be no doubt that a much more efficient airline sector now exists, to a large extent the result of effective competition from low cost new entrants. With few exceptions however, these catalysts have had only short lives. The restructuring process triggered by the removal of economic controls is as yet incomplete. As this phase draws to a conclusion there is a strong possibility that the survivors will increasingly acknowledge the futility of further competitive rivalry, with the result that the choice that consumers will be presented with will be extremely limited. That one still may have a choice to make is not at issue, what is in question is how significant this may actually be. In the longer term, perhaps the most important lesson to have been gained from deregulation will be that complete economic freedom does not necessarily guarantee a strongly competitive environment.

APPENDICES

Appendix 1   Directory of US Passenger Carriers

(In 1981 the CAB began classifying airlines on the basis of annual revenues, categorising 'Major' carriers as those generating in excess of $1 billion and 'National' carriers as earning between $100 million and $1 billion.)

AirCal, known until 1981 as Air California, was acquired by American in 1986 and absorbed in 1987. The airline began operations from Orange County Airport in 1967 specialising in high frequency, single class scheduled services within the State of California. Following deregulation the carrier extended its route network to other Western states.

Air Wisconsin, which was acquired by United in January 1992, has recently been disposed of by its parent company. The airline had been functioning as a feeder carrier for United at Chicago and Washington (Dulles) since 1986. The company began scheduled commuter operations in 1965 and expanded to jet service in 1983. In the early 1990s it provided scheduled services to some 31 cities in the US Midwest, using a fleet of 36 aircraft.

Alaska, currently the largest National airline, is now the dominant carrier along the US West Coast. It operates an extensive network of scheduled services throughout Alaska and the Western Seaboard of North America, including Mexico. The airline, originally founded in 1932, acquired the name Alaska in 1944 following several mergers with smaller firms. Horizon Air, a Seattle based regional carrier, was purchased by Alaska's parent company in 1986. Jet America, a Long Beach based new entrant, was also acquired in 1986 and merged in 1987. A fleet of 68 jet aircraft are currently operated.

Aloha, founded in 1946, operates a network of scheduled services in the Hawaiian Islands. It is currently the eigth largest National carrier and operates a fleet of 18 jet aircraft.

American, founded in 1934 and currently second largest of the megacarriers, operates an extensive network of scheduled services throughout the US and to over 70 destinations worldwide. The airline concentrates its domestic operations at five hubs: Chicago, Dallas, Nashville, Raleigh/Durham and San Juan. An extensive network of feeder services is provided under the name 'American Eagle'. In 1986 the carrier acquired AirCal, providing it with a large West Coast network of routes. Considerable international expansion has occurred over the past decade. In 1991 the airline acquired a number of transatlantic routes from TWA. A fleet of 680 jet aircraft is operated, with some 96,000 staff employed. America's parent company, AMR, owns the Sabre CRS.

America West, the last surviving new entrant of any size and one of the country's Majors, filed for Chapter 11 bankruptcy protection in June 1991. The airline commenced operations in 1983 and has since developed a network of domestic services based on hubs at Las Vegas and Phoenix. Its one international route, from Honolulu to Nagoya (Tokyo), was sold off in 1992 to Northwest. A fleet of 85 jet aircraft is currently operated.

Braniff, a former trunk carrier originally established in 1928, encountered severe financial difficulties during the early days of deregulation and ceased trading in 1982. In addition to domestic services, an extensive South American route network had been operated. The carrier was reactivated on a much smaller scale in 1984, operating a network of domestic services from hubs at Dallas and Kansas City. This venture experienced considerable competition from the two megacarriers also with hubs at Dallas and ceased operations in November 1989. A third attempt to operate scheduled services under the Braniff name (Braniff International) was initiated in 1991 using a small fleet of aircraft, but this too ended in failure.

Continental, currently the sixth largest airline, emerged from its second period operating under Chapter 11 bankruptcy protection in May 1993 with Air Canada and Air Partners, a Texas-based partnership, acquiring a majority shareholding in the company. A former trunk carrier originally established in 1934, Continental was purchased by Texas Air in 1981, the parent company of Texas International. The two airlines were merged in 1982 retaining the Continental name. In 1983 the airline filed for Chapter 11 bankruptcy protection as a revolutionary means by which to reduce its labour costs. A reorganisation plan was filed with Bankruptcy Court in 1985 and the airline emerged from Chapter 11 protection a year later. Today an extensive domestic network is operated using four major hubs located at Cleveland, Denver, Houston and Newark. The carrier has recently contracted its network of transpacific routes. Transatlantic services are operated to France, Germany, Spain and the UK. A network of domestic feeder services are provided under the title 'Continental Express'. The carrier currently employs 40,000 staff and has a fleet of 300 aircraft.

Delta, the country's third largest megacarrier, expanded its international network of services in 1991 by taking over Pan Am's remaining transatlantic routes. The company also acquired the failed airline's domestic Shuttle operation and its extensive inter-European network. A large domestic route system is operated from six hubs located at Atlanta, Cincinnati, Dallas, Los Angeles, Orlando and Salt Lake City. International services are operated to 33 countries around the globe. The company acquired Western A/l, another former trunk carrier, in 1986. Traditionally the most conservative of the 'big three', the airline has nonetheless been highly successful, currently employing some 74,000 staff and utilising 560 jet aircraft. A domestic feeder network is operated under the 'Delta Connection' banner.

Eastern, formerly one of the country's largest carriers, ceased operations in January 1991. The airline was acquired by Texas Air Corporation in 1986, owners of Continental. An extensive network of domestic services had been operated in addition to routes to the Carribbean and South America.

Frontier, a former local service carrier formed in 1946, was acquired by People Express in 1985. Until its closure in 1986 the airline had operated a large network of services to 22 US states, Canada and Mexico from its Denver base.

Hawaiian, the country's third largest National carrier, operates a network of services throughout the Hawaiian Islands and across the Pacific. A fleet of 28 aircraft is currently operated.

Horizon, based in Seattle, provides a network of feeder services throughout the Pacific Northwest. The airline was established in 1981 and acquired by the Alaska Air Group, owners of Alaska, in 1986. A fleet of 58 aircraft is currently operated.

Hughes Airwest, formed in 1968 and acquired by the Hughes Corporation in 1970, was acquired by Republic in 1980. A large network of services had been operated throughout the Western states.

Jet America, one of the new entrants under deregulation, commenced operations in 1981 from Long Beach. The carrier operated a small fleet of MD-82 aircraft, but was acquired by the Alaska Air Group in 1986 and merged with Alaska.

Kiwi Int. A/l, a new entrant carrier formed in 1992 by ex-employees of Eastern and Pan Am, operates a network of low fare services from Newark using a fleet of eight aircraft.

Markair, based in Anchorage, entered Chapter 11 bankruptcy protection in June 1991. The carrier operates a network of services to other US states and within Alaska. Originally formed in 1946, the company assumed its present name in 1984. A fleet of thirteen jet aircraft is currently operated.

Midway, one of the longest surviving new entrants, finally succumbed in November 1991. Formed in 1979 and based at Chicago's downtown Midway airport, the carrier had grown steadily throughout the 1980s. Its decision to establish a second hub at Philadelphia in 1991 during a time of national recession proved fatal.

Midwest Express, a subsidiary company of Kimberly-Clark established in 1984, has been operating a growing network of services from its Milwaukee hub. The airline operates a fleet of 17 jet aircraft.

National was acquired by Pan Am in 1980 and its operations absorbed. With the advent of deregulation the trunk carrier had began operating transatlantic services from its Miami hub. An extensive domestic network of services was also provided. The purchase of National marked the beginning of Pan Am's long period of financial difficulties culminating in its ultimate demise.

North Central, a local service carrier established in 1944, merged with Southern in 1979 to form Republic. The airline had operated services to fourteen states from its base at Minneapolis.

Northwest, formerly known as Northwest Orient and now fourth largest of the megacarriers, operates a sizeable network of transpacific routes. The former trunk carrier was first established in 1926. To increase the airline's network of domestic routes Republic, also based at Minneapolis, was acquired in 1986. Transatlantic services are provided to France, Germany, Holland and the UK. KLM acquired a 20% shareholding in NWA Inc., the airline's parent company, in 1990. A network of commuter feeder services are operated in the US under the name 'Northwest Airlink'. A fleet of 360 aircraft is currently operated.

Ozark, a former local service carrier based in St. Louis, was acquired by TWA in 1986. At the time of its acquisition the airline operated a fleet of 50 jet aircraft to 66 cities in 25 states. The company was first established in 1943.

Pacific Southwest operated a network of high frequency, low fare services to 30 cities located in California and six other Western states until it was acquired by

USAir in 1987. The former intrastate carrier was first established in 1949. At the time of its acquisition the airline operated a fleet of 55 jet aircraft.

Pan Am, the US flag carrier for many decades, finally succumbed to financial pressures in 1991. Ever since its acquisition of National in 1980 the airline had experienced difficulties. Most of the company's international services were centred on New York, whilst the focus of National's domestic operations was Miami. Pan Am had only survived the 1980s by selling off various of its assets to other carriers. First established in 1927 the carrier in its heyday had operated a round the world network of services.

People Express, largest of the new entrants and most cited as vindicating deregulation of the industry, was acquired by Texas Air in 1986. The airline was formed in 1980 and grew rapidly to operate an extensive domestic network of high frequency, low fare, no frills services based on its Newark hub. A service to London (Gatwick) was also operated from 1983. At the time of its acquisition the company employed 5000 staff and operated a fleet of 60 jet aircraft.

Piedmont, a former local service carrier, was acquired by USAir in 1988 and its operations absorbed a year later. An extensive network of domestic services was operated based on the carrier's hubs at Charlotte, Baltimore and Dayton. In addition the airline began operating an international service to London (Gatwick) from Charlotte in 1988. At the time of its acquisition the company employed a staff of 15,000 and operated a fleet of 160 jet aircraft.

Reno Air began scheduled operations in 1992. The carrier operates a number of services to neighbouring states from its Reno hub using a fleet of seven jet aircraft.

Republic was formed in 1979 through the merger of North Central and Southern. Until its acquisition in 1986 by Northwest the airline operated a large domestic network serving some 100 cities in 32 states. At the time of its absorption into Northwest the company was employing 13500 staff and operating 168 aircraft.

Southern, a former local service carrier based in Atlanta and established in 1949, merged with North Central in 1979 to form Republic.

Southwest, formed in 1967 to provide low fare services within Texas, has grown steadily to achieve Major status and is now the only really successful new entrant to the interstate markets. A fleet of 157 Boeing 737 aircraft are used to provide a network of mostly short haul, low fare, single class, high frequency services to 15 states. With among the lowest operating costs of any scheduled operator the company has been consistently profitable over the past two decades. Most recently the airline has stepped in to operate services from Chicago (Midway) after the demise of Midway. The carrier currently has 14000 employees.

Texas Air, originally the parent company of Texas International, acquired a large number of airlines during the early and mid 1980s to become by 1986 the largest airline group in the US. In 1982 the group acquired a controlling interest in Continental and merged the two carriers. Eastern was acquired by the group in 1986, as was People Express. Eastern and Continental were kept as separate operations throughout their period of ownership by Texas Air. Mounting financial difficulties ultimately led to the demise of Eastern in 1991 and Continental's filing for bankruptcy protection a year earlier.

Texas International, a former intrastate carrier owned by Texas Air, was merged with Continental in 1982.

Trump Shuttle acquired Eastern's Boston - New York - Washington shuttle operation in 1988. (Eastern had previously provided the shuttle for 27 years.) Services commenced in 1989 using 21 former Eastern aircraft. In 1991, owing to owner Donald Trump's financial difficulties, USAir acquired the right to operate the shuttle service. Flights are now operated under the title USAir Shuttle. USAir has an option to purchase the shuttle operation, now owned by a consortium of banks, in 1995.

TWA, formerly one of the US's major international carriers, emerged from Chapter 11 bankruptcy protection in November 1993. The airline has experienced severe financial difficulties in recent years and has been forced to sell off many of its assets. Most significant have been its sales to American and USAir of several transatlantic routes. The carrier continues to operate a large domestic network of services from its main hub at St. Louis, but its international operations are now comparatively small. The airline's 26000 employees now have a 45% shareholding in the company. A fleet of 180 aircraft is currently operated.

United, formerly the biggest trunk airline and now largest of the megacarriers, has considerably expanded its international route network over the past two years. In 1990 the airline purchased Pan Am's transatlantic routes to London (Heathrow), whilst in 1991 the Latin American routes of the same carrier were acquired. An extensive domestic network is operated which involves the use of four main hubs at Chicago, Denver, San Francisco and Washington (Dulles). A large network of transpacific routes is also operated, the company having acquired Pan Am's pacific division in 1986. A domestic commuter feeder network is provided under the name 'United Express'. Over 83,000 staff are currently employed and a fleet of 540 jet aircraft operated. 50% of the airline's CRS, Covia (formerly known as Apollo), was sold to a consortium of European airlines in 1988. In 1992 it was announced that Covia was to be merged with the European CRS Galileo.

USAir, sixth largest Major carrier, acquired Piedmont and PSA in 1987. An extensive network of domestic services is operated using traffic hubs located at Baltimore, Charlotte, Pittsburgh and Philadelphia. In 1992 the airline acquired two of TWA's transatlantic routes to London (Gatwick). British Airways acquired a 25% shareholding in the company in 1993, attracted by the feeder potential of the carrier's large domestic network. The airline currently employs a staff of 46,000 and operates a fleet of 440 jet aircraft.

WestAir, a regional commuter airline based in California, is a wholly owned subsidiary of Mesa Airlines. In 1991 the carrier sold its Atlantic Coast division prior to its acquisition by Mesa, another commuter carrier based in New Mexico. Since 1986 the company has operated as a commuter feeder carrier for United.

Western, a former trunk airline, was acquired by Delta in 1986. The carrier had operated an extensive network of services from its traffic hub at Salt Lake City throughout the Western states and to Hawaii and Mexico. A fleet of 80 jet aircraft were in use when the carrier's operations were absorbed by Delta in 1987.

An early defensive strategy to be adopted by the majority of established US carriers involved them restructuring their routes into hub and spoke networks. By concentrating operations at hubs, airlines made access to these points expensive, if not impossible, for aspiring new entrants. Considerable economies were derived from this reorganisation of routes, especially when supported by a dominance of company owned computer reservation terminals in the major traffic generating travel agencies surrounding the hub.

In order to able to be able to derive the most benefit from this new system however the operation of more than one hub was required. Developing a new hub could be time consuming, expensive and risky. Acquiring one by taking over or merging with another airline had the double advantage of providing an already successfully established hub and eliminating a former competitor. Merger mania thus became a second important phase in the process of organisational change following deregulation.

As mergers concentrate market power the prospect of such action being used to exploit consumers or unfairly disadvantage competitors is increased. Ordinarily in the US matters relating to such issues would be referred to the Antitrust Divisions of the Department of Justice (DoJ). However in the case of air transport the Civil Aeronautics Board (CAB) had been the responsible agency, providing carriers with a considerable degree of immunity from antitrust legislation. On the demise of CAB, responsibility for this passed to the Department of Transportation (DoT). Considerable debate had taken place as to whether such matters should rightly have been under the jurisdiction of the DoJ. In the event the acknowledged expertise of the DoT in matters of transportation proved decisive. Despite this demarcation both departments have made recommendations about each of the major airline merger proposals.

The most recent airline merger case, that of USAir and Piedmont Airlines, is interesting in that it throws into sharp focus many of the complex issues that governments face when deciding on policy relating to market intervention. The DoJ, with reference to the Hirschman Herfindahl Index (HHI)[1], argued that as the domestic airline industry system wide showed only a moderate degree of concentration the merger should be approved. The index takes into consideration both the number of carriers operating in a particular market and their relative traffic shares, and is calculated by summing the square of each carrier's market share. A summary measurement is thus provided, its relative simplicity making it an attractive measure to adopt. However, although it provides a reasonable method of measuring changes in market concentration it provides no insight as to the ways in which firms are most likely to use their greater market power. The simple example given below illustrates this.

The table gives details of the traffic shares of airlines operating in three markets, whilst the graph shows the cumulative concentration curve for each market.

Table A.2.1 **Traffic Shares (%)**

Market	Firm 1	Firm 2	Firm 3	Firm 4	Firm 5	HHI
A	50	50				5000
B	65	15	10	10		4650
C	60	25	5	5	5	4300

The duopolistic market is shown as having the highest degree of concentration. However, assuming that these firms do not collude, it is possible that the dominant firm in market B may be able to exert sufficient control over its competitors that it is able to force consumers to pay higher prices than they would in market A for comparable journeys. By contrast if firm 2 in market C is in some way contractually tied to firm 1, as in the role of a feeder operator, this market may be more likely to exhibit less competition.

Figure A.2.1 Cummulative Concentration Curves for Each Market

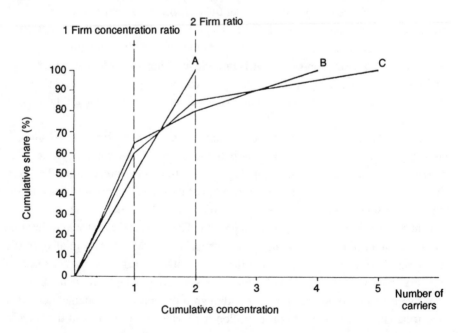

The degree of collusion between carriers is an aspect of oligopolistic markets that neither the HHI, nor indeed any other concentration measure, can take adequately into account. Such measures in practice can only sensibly be employed to provide a rough guide as to when an in-depth appraisal of a proposed merger is advisable. Choosing an appropriate trigger level then becomes the crucial concern. This can only realistically be determined after a detailed examination of the behaviour of firms in a large number of markets exhibiting varying degrees of concentration. The DoJ for its purposes has adopted the following convention: HHI valuations of less than 1000 are interpreted as indicating low levels of concentration; values of between 1000 and 1800 as showing moderate concentration; and values of over 1800 as demonstrating high concentration. The fact that system wide the US domestic airline industry exhibited an HHI of only 1303 in 1987 (842 in 1977) was a key factor in the decision to allow the USAir-Piedmont merger to proceed.

However at the micro level many of the individual city-pairs operated by these two carriers showed very high levels of concentration. Given the high degree of commonality of routes operated by both companies it seems to have been highly inappropriate to have assessed the pros and cons of this particular merger proposal using an industry wide measure of concentration. The higher than average net yields earned by the two airlines can only be explained by their adoption of near monopoly prices, given their near industry average costs and lack of an in-house CRS. The view that the merger would be most likely to result in greater exploitation of consumers was expounded by DoT Administrative Law Judge Ronnie Yoder. He advised against approval, but this recommendation was officially overruled a month later by the DoT.

The DoJ's 1982 guidelines on horizontal mergers are in the words of Steven Salop '...built on the premise that collusion... is less likely to succeed in less concentrated markets, in markets where few entry barriers exist, and in markets where competitive price cuts are more difficult for rivals to detect quickly'.[2] Substantial entry barriers do however exist in today's airline markets. Carriers have expended considerable time, money and imagination in their establishment. The view expounded by many economists before and during the early days of deregulation that airline markets could be expected to exhibit high degrees of contestability has not proved to be the case. In the circumstances it is difficult not to draw the conclusion that the real reason for the DoT allowing the merger rested on the view that it would be better in the long term to have seven megacarriers rather than six.[3]

Future debate about airline regulation will increasingly focus on issues concerned with obtaining a more equitable distribution of the benefits that a more efficiently organised industry has brought. Successful carriers have adopted strategies that have been aimed at increasing their competitive advantage. Achieving this objective provides them with the ability to organise their markets leading to still greater competitive advantage. Monopoly or collusive oligopoly is the end result of this process, as we are increasingly witnessing in the US. Wresting control of airline markets from an increasingly powerful group of carriers is likely to be an expensive and highly controversial further phase in the process of 'deregulation'. Given the inefficiencies produced by earlier attempts at regulating the industry, the onus will be on governments to establish convincingly when campaigning for reregulation that on balance any benefits likely to be derived will outweigh the costs of implementing such a policy.

Notes

1. The formula for the HHI is: $H = \sum_{i=1}^{n} s_i^2$ where s is the traffic share of the i'th carrier, and n represents the total number of operators in the specific market. The usual convention is to measure market share as a proportion resulting in index values of between 0 and 1, but in the US percentages have been adopted producing valuations of between 0 and 10,000.
2. Salop, Steven C. (1987), 'Symposium on Mergers and Antitrust', Journal of Economic Perspectives, Fall, pp. 3-12.
3. The seven carriers and their respective market shares in 1988 were: Texas Air Corporation (Continental and Eastern) 18.8%, United 16.8%, American 16.3%, Delta 13.6%, Northwest 7.1%, TWA 6.2% and USAir/Piedmont 9.1%.

Appendix 3   Western Europe's Passenger Airline Industry - A Summary

Scheduled Carrier(s)	Charter Carrier(s)	Alliances

Austria

Austrian A/l
(52% state-owned)
four A310, 7 MD-81,
five MD-87, 6 MD-82,
two MD-83.
Austrian Air Services
(100% owned by *Austrian*)
fleet: 7 Fokker 50.
Rheintalflug
three Dash 8.
Tyrolean A/w
two Dash 7, 16 Dash 8.

Lauda Air
(26% owned by *Lufthansa*)
two 737-300, two
737-400, four
767-300ER.

Swissair has a 10%
shareholding in
Austrian, All Nippon
has 9% and *Air
France* 1.5%.

Belgium

Delta AT
(79% owned by *Sabena*)
three F28, five BAe 146,
9 Brasilia.
Sabena
(25% state-owned)
two 747-300, one 747-100,
two DC-10, three A310,
ten 737-200, six 737-300,
three 737-400, six 737-500.
VLM
three Fokker 50.

Air Belgium Int.
one 757, one 737-400.
EuroBelgian A/l
five 737-300, one 737-400.
European A/l
three A300.
Sobelair
(100% owned by *Sabena*)
five 737-200, one 737-300,
two 737-400.

Air France has a 35%
shareholding in
Sabena.

Denmark

Cimber Air Denmark
two F.28, 8 ATR 42.
Maersk Air
13 737-300, five 737-500,
8 Fokker 50.

Premiair
four DC-10, four A320.

Maersk Air's UK
subsidiary operates
services from
Birmingham on behalf

175

Scheduled Carrier(s)	Charter Carrier(s)	Alliances

Muk Air
one Shorts 360, two Shorts 330,
four Bandeirante.
SAS (see Sweden)
(50% state-owned jointly by
Denmark, Norway &
Sweden)

of *British A/w.*

France

Air France
(96% state-owned)
7 Concorde, 14 747-400,
two 747-300, 24 747-200,
13 747-100, 16 737-200,
three 737-300, 16 737-500,
five DC-10, nine A300,
8 A340, 11 A310,
25 A320.
Air Inter
(72% owned by *Air France*)
22 A300, three A330,
32 A320, 9 Mercure.
Air Littoral
(subsidiary of *Euralair*;
operates for *Air France*)
two ATR 72, five ATR 42,
10 Brasilia.
Brit Air
(operates services on
behalf of *Air France*)
three ATR 72, 11 ATR 42,
six Saab 340.
Regional A/l
five Saab 340, 6 Jetstream,
six Metro.

Air Charter
(80% owned by *Air France*)
two A300, four 727-200,
8 737-200, one 737-500.
Air Liberte
seven MD-83, two A300,
one A310, one 747-100.
Air Provence
two Caravelle 12,
9 Gulfstream.
Air Toulouse
three Caravelle 10.
AOM French
five MD-83, 7 DC-10.
Corsair Int.
two 747-100, one 747-200,
two 737-400.
Corse Mediterreanee
two F-100, 8 ATR 72.
Euralair
two 727, five 737-200,
three 737-500.
Europe Aero Service
two 727-200, six 737-200,
two 737-300, one 737-500.
7 Caravelle 10.

Air France and
Lufthansa have
formed a major
strategic alliance.

176

Scheduled Carrier(s)	**Charter Carrier(s)**	**Alliances**

TAT European A/l
(50% owned by *British A/w*)
23 F28, 14 Fokker 100,
eight ATR 72, 11 ATR 42,
two 737-200, two Brasilia.

TEA France
one 737-300.

Germany

Contactair
(operates on behalf of
Lufthansa CityLine)
six Dash 8, two Jetstream.
Conti-Flug
two BAe 146.
Deutsche BA
(49% owned by *British A/w*)
seven 737-300, 9 Saab 340.
EuroBerlin
(51% owned by *Air France*;
49% by *Lufthansa*)
six 737-300.
Eurowings
19 ATR 42, 8 ATR 72.
Hamburg A/l
7 Dash 8.
Interot A/w
four Dash 8.
Lufthansa
(51% state-owned)
17 747-400, eight 747-200,
six DC-10, ten A340,
11 A300, 12 A310,
33 A320, two A321,
six 737-400, 43 737-300,
31 737-500, 30 737-200.
Lufthansa CityLine
(100% owned by *Lufthansa*)
25 Fokker 50, 13 Canadair RJ.

Aero Lloyd
13 MD-83, four MD-87,
three DC-9.
Air Berlin
five 737-400.
Condor
(100% owned by *Lufthansa*;
aircraft operated by *Suedflug*)
19 757, six 767-300ER,
three DC-10, five 737-300.
Germania
ten 737-300.
Hapag Lloyd
7 A310, nine 737-400,
four 737-500.
LTU
four MD-11, nine L-1011.
LTU Sud Int.
four 767-300ER, seven 757.

Lufthansa and *Air
France* have formed a
major strategic
alliance.

Scheduled Carrier(s)	**Charter Carrier(s)**	**Alliances**

WDL
seven F-27.

Greece
Olympic
(100% state-owned)
four 747-200, ten A300,
11 737- 200, 6 737-400.
Olympic Aviation
(100% owned by *Olympic*)
five ATR 72, four ATR 42,
5 Shorts 330, 7 Dornier 228.
South East European
(associate of *Virgin Atlantic*)
one 737-400.

Venus
two MD-87.

Ireland
Aer Lingus
(100% state-owned)
three 747-100, 6 737-400,
nine 737-500.
Aer Lingus Commuter
(100% owned by *Aer Lingus*)
6 Fokker 50, four Saab 340.
Cityjet
(associate of *Virgin Atlantic*)
three BAe 146.
Ryanair
eight 737-200.

TransLift
two DC-8, one A320.

Italy
Air Dolomiti
three Dash 8.
ATI
(100% owned by *Alitalia*)
36 MD-82, four DC-9.

Air Europe Italy
(27% owned by *Alitalia*)
four 767-300ER.
Eurofly
(45% owned by *Alitalia*)
three DC-9.

Scheduled Carrier(s)	Charter Carrier(s)	Alliances

Alitalia
(85% state-owned)
14 747-200, 6 MD-11,
14 A300, 42 MD-82, 34 DC-9.
Avianova
(100% owned by *ATI*)
11 ATR 42.
Meridiana
8 MD-82, 6 DC-9,
four BAe 146.
TAS A/w
two BAe 146.

Lauda Air Spa
(subsidiary of *Lauda Air*)
one 767-300ER.

Luxemburg
Luxair
(23% state-owned)
one 747SP, two 737-400,
two 737-500, four Fokker 50,
three Brasilia.

Lufthansa has a
13% shareholding in
Luxair.

Netherlands
Air Exel Commuter
three Brasilia.
BASE Business A/l
three Jetstream.
Flexair
one Dornier 228.
KLM
(38% state-owned)
16 747-400, three 747-300,
ten 747-200, four DC10,
two MD-11, eight A310,
13 737-300, 12 737-400.
KLM Cityhopper
(100% owned by *KLM*)
four F-28, 10 Fokker 50,
12 Saab 340.

Air Holland Charter
two 757, one 737-400.
Martinair
(34% owned by *KLM*
three 747-200, five 737-300ER,
three DC-10, one A310.
Transavia
(80% owned by *KLM*)
two 757, eight 737-300,
five 737-200.

Scheduled Carrier(s)	**Charter Carrier(s)**	**Alliances**

Norway

Braathens
six 737-400, 16 737-500,
eight 737-200.
SAS (see Sweden)
(50% state-owned jointly by
Denmark, Norway & Sweden)
Wideroe
(partly owned by *Braathens*
and *SAS*)
8 Dash 7, six Dash 8,
three Brasilia, 12 Twin Otter.

Norwegian Air Shuttle
(100% owned by *Braathens*)
five Fokker 50, ten F.27.

Portugal

EuroAir
(30% owned by*TAP*)
three Dornier 228.
Portugalia
four F-100.
TAP - Air Portugal
(100% state-owned)
7 L-1011, five A310,
10 737-300, 10 737-200,
six A320.

Air Columbus
three 737-300.

Spain

Aviaco
(33% owned by *Iberia*)
13 MD-88, 18 DC-9.
Binter Canarias
(subsidiary of *Iberia*)
six ATR 72, four CN235.
Binter Mediterranea
(subsidiary of *Iberia*)
five CN235.

Air Europa
four 757, 12 737-300.
Centennial
two MD-83.
Futura
(25% owned by *Aer Lingus*)
six 737-400, two 737-300.
LTE Int.
(100% owned by *LTU*)
five 757.

Scheduled Carrier(s)	**Charter Carrier(s)**	**Alliances**

Iberia
(100% state-owned)
7 747-200, eight DC-10,
8 A300, 22 A320,
30 727-200, 24 MD-87,
three 757.
VIVA Air
(96% owned by *Iberia*)
nine 737-300.

Oasis Int. A/l
one A310, five MD-83,
one MD-82.
Spanair
(49% owned by *SAS*)
two 767-300ER, 9 MD-83.

Sweden

Air Nordic
five F-27.
Golden Air
(subsidiary of *Skyways*)
four Saab 340.
Holmstroem Air
three Shorts 360,
three Dornier 228.
Malmo Aviation
eight BAe 146.
SAS
(50% state-owned jointly by
Denmark, Norway & Sweden)
13 767-300ER, 15 MD-82,
33 MD-81, 17 MD-87,
33 DC-9, 10 737-500,
19 F-28.
SAS Commuter
(100% owned by *SAS*)
22 Fokker 50, 8 Saab 340.
Skyways
7 Saab 340, one Shorts 360.
Transwede
five MD-83, two MD-87,
five F-100.

Falcon Aviation
three 737-300.
Nordic East A/l
one DC-8, one MD-82,
one 737-200.

Scheduled Carrier(s)	Charter Carrier(s)	Alliances

Switzerland

Air Engiadina
one Dornier 328, one
Dornier 228, one Jetstream.
Crossair
(56% owned by *Swissair*)
five BAe 146, 23 Saab 340,
five Fokker 50.
Swissair
five 747-300, 12 MD-11,
ten A310, 24 MD-81,
ten Fokker 100.

Air Starline
one DC-8.
Balair/CTA
(57% owned by *Swissair*)
three A310, three MD-82,
two MD-83, four MD-87.
TEA Basel
five 737-300.

United Kingdom

Air UK
(15% owned by *KLM)*
eight BAe 146, five F-100,
14 F-27, one
Shorts 360.
Aurigny
one Shorts 360,
nine Trislander.
British Airways
seven Concorde,
26 747-400, 16 747-200,
15 747-100, seven DC-10,
21 767-300, 42 757,
35 737-400, 39 737-200,
ten A320, 14 BAe ATP.
British Midland
(35% owned by *SAS*)
six 737-400, six 737-300,
three 737-500, 13 DC-9.
Business Air
one BAe 146, six Saab 340,
one Shorts 360.

Air 2000
15 757, four A320.
Air Bristol
two BAC 1-11.
Airtours Int.
two 767-300ER, ten MD-83,
two 757, two A320.
Air UK Leisure
(30% owned by *Air UK*)
seven 737-400.
Ambassador
two 757.
Britannia A/w
10 767-200, 19 757.
British World A/l
two BAe 146, six BAC 1-11,
nine Viscount.
Caledonian A/w
(100% owned by *British A/w*)
six Tristar, six 757,
one DC-10.
Excalibur A/w
four A320.

Scheduled Carrier(s)	Charter Carrier(s)	Alliances

Brymon Aviation
(100% owned by
British A/w)
six Dash 7, four Dash 8.
Cityflyer Express
(operates in association
with *British A/w)*
5 ATR 42, 3 Shorts 360.
Gill Air
one ATR 42, three Shorts 360,
8 Shorts 330.
Jersey European A/w
three BAe 146, 8 F-27,
four Shorts 360.
Loganair
(part of the Airlines of
Britain Group, owners of
British Midland)
5 Shorts 360, five Islander,
three Jetstream 31.
Maersk Air UK
(subsidiary of *Maersk Air*;
operates on behalf of
British A/w)
6 BAC 1-11, three Jetstream.
Manx A/l
(part of the Airlines of
Britain Group, owners of
British Midland)
two BAe 146, ten BAe ATP,
3 Shorts 360, 8 Jetstream 41.
Virgin Atlantic
7 747-200, one 747-100,
four A340.

Leisure Int. A/w
(subsidiary of
Air UK Leisure)
two 767-300ER.
Monarch
four A300, eight 757,
six 737-300, five A320.

Appendix 4   The Experience of Other Heavily Regulated UK Industries with Deregulation

Regulation of public enterprise in the UK, in the words of Kay and Vickers (1988), has...'always been vague, ill-defined, and subject to political influence'. It has not proved possible, it would seem, to establish a coherent framework of economic control. In order to overcome this failure the Treasury sought to limit the financial requirements of such industries. In addition, in-depth monitoring exercises were undertaken from time to time, which had the effect of creating atmospheres of mistrust on both sides.[1] The managers of public enterprises considered themselves to be shackled and unable to act in a commercial way.[2] The change of government in 1979 heralded the introduction of a major evaluation of regulatory policy, with a strong emphasis being placed on creating competitive markets wherever it was feasible to do so.

Attempts to introduce the rigours of the market place into industries previously granted immunity from such discomfiture have taken many different forms. One key area of interest to the UK Government over the past decade in this regard has been the nationalised industries, many of which have occupied positions of monopoly. Aside from reasons dictated by political dogma, a primary objective has been to make these industries operate more efficiently. Privatisation, it has been argued, is an essential prerequisite to the engendering of a competitive environment within such industries. The monopolistic nature of many of the firms that have been privatised though have necessitated government finding additional, more direct, means by which to introduce an element of rivalry. Privately owned monopolistic firms have more to gain from the exploitation of market power than their publicly owned counterparts, as their shareholders and managers can benefit through greater dividends and more attractive emoluments respectively. Any ensuing efficiency gains therefore would be unlikely to be passed on to consumers, as without the threat of a competitor such action could in no way benefit the firm. Outrageous behaviour, of course, would provoke an adverse response from government, but it would be unlikely that such a firm would be so foolish as to act in such a manner. The lobbying of Ministers and other well tried techniques aimed at massaging public opinion could be expected to play a key role in the safeguarding of the monopolist's image.

Injecting competition into industries formerly controlled by state owned monopolies has proved to be both controversial and technically difficult. The successful privatisation of such firms has rested in large measure on their being able to retain their positions of market dominance. The granting by government of special concessions to new entrants in order to allow time for them to establish themselves has been greeted by the Directors of privatised companies with disdain and, on occasion, outrage. The comments made in 1989 by the Chairman of British Telecommunications (BT) in his annual report to shareholders aptly demonstrates this viewpoint. 'Provided the authorities can establish a regulatory framework that balances fairly the needs of domestic competition policy with the broader international perspective, I know that we can achieve our stated goal of becoming the leading telecommunications company worldwide.'[3] Whilst this particular company could be expected to face competition in any overseas markets it wished to enter, the provision of a restraining influence in its home territory has necessitated the government artificially creating one. This has been attempted in two ways: firstly by abolishing BT's exclusive privileges in the telecommunications sector and secondly by creating OFTEL to regulate the industry.

The structural approach adopted by earlier governments as a means by which to regulate naturally monopolistic industries has been replaced by various forms of behavioural control.[4] The measures employed have varied between industries, with each allegedly tailor made to suit the particular characteristics of of the market place. The public utilities have proved especially difficult in this regard, as the social objectives pursued by many of these concerns often have been incompatible with more narrowly defined commercial goals. For example, the provision of telephone services at a standard charge irrespective of geographical location has involved a considerable element of cross-subsidisation. Attempting to preserve this type of public welfare consideration, whilst simultaneously encouraging the industry to operate on a purely commercial basis, has necessitated the delicate balancing of two totally conflicting objectives. Not surprisingly, the Chairmen of such enterprises find these requirements difficult to reconcile. In these circumstances many observers would argue that the social objective in practice would be awarded a lower priority and in the longer term be quietly forgotten about.

In order to illustrate some of the difficulties likely to be encountered in the removal of economic controls governing former state owned monopolistic industries, the recent experiences of the UK telecommunications, gas, local stage carriage and television sectors are outlined below.

A.4.1 Telecommunications

As regards telecommunications, BT was privatised in 1984. The move towards privatising the industry had commenced in 1981 when the Post Office was divested of its telecommunication interests. An Act of Parliament the same year introduced

some liberalisation measures to the industry in terms of the supply of telecommunications apparatus.[5] The public announcement about the sale of BT came in 1982 and triggered a debate about the possible abuse of its monopoly power. The Littlechild Report into this matter was published a year later and recommended the introduction of a pricing control mechanism generally known as RPI - X.[6] The method required that a weighted average of the prices of BT's regulated services should fall by a minimum of X% annually in real terms over a five year period. X was set at 3 when privatisation occurred in 1984 and covered around 50% of its revenues. The regulatory approach adopted in this industry formed the model for later privatisations and is described below.

Regulatory control of telecommunications is shared by three parties: OFTEL, which monitors compliance with licence conditions and protects the interests of consumers; the Monopolies and Mergers Commission (MMC), which determines future price controls governing the industry after the initial five year period and arbitrates in disputes about changes in the conditions imposed in licences; and the relevant government Minister, who is responsible for the granting of licences. In addition, the Office of Fair Trading (OFT) has powers in matters of competition policy. Within this framework considerable scope exists for the regulatory authority to exercise its own discretion as to precisely how, and in what areas, to concentrate its activities. OFTEL, for example, has concentrated particularly on promoting competition and protecting consumers' interests.[7] 'For consumers and others concerned with competition, it is a matter of good fortune, rather than legislative design, that Professor Carsberg and his team have chosen to give a high priority to the promotion of competition, and have skilfully pursued that end.'[8]

A.4.2 Gas

OFGAS, the regulatory authority set up to monitor and control the activities of the privatised British Gas (BG), has faced considerably more difficulty in its attempts to check the company's compliance with price controls. Despite its diverse interests BG is required only to provide accounting information for its gas supply business in aggregate. The fact that the OFT became involved in conducting an investigation into BG's industrial users' pricing policies following complaints by consumers would tend to point to an inherent weakness in the way OFGAS has been able to carry out its functions. A significant factor here concerns the fact that the enterprise was privatised intact as a horizontally and vertically integrated monopoly. In the case of BT, Mercury provided a yardstick by which to compare both efficiency and prices, but in the case of the gas industry no such strictly comparable option exists.

A.4.3 Bus Services

The approach adopted in the bus industry has been very different from that used for the telecommunication and gas industries. Local stage carriage services have been for many years loss making activities and as a consequence have been subject to both direct subsidy and cross-subsidisation. The 1968 Transport Act introduced the system of direct subsidy provision for unremunerative bus and rail services, following an almost continuing decline in public transport patronage. The bus industry had been tightly regulated in 1930, when a licensing system had been introduced for stage carriage services in order to limit market entry and improve safety standards. A newly formed body of traffic commissioners were to organise and regulate the awarding of route licences. Under this regime the practice of using profits earned on more highly trafficked routes to cover the losses incurred on lightly loaded journeys developed and eventually lead to the emergence of an industry characterised by area monopoly. By the 1960's, with dwindling profits the practice was becoming less and less viable, hence the introduction of direct subvention.

The low traffic levels in many areas rendered the provision of stage carriage services by more than one company an unnecessary extravagance. Local authorities have been responsible since 1974 for the provision of direct subsidies to bus companies in order to maintain socially necessary services. Two approaches have been advocated as a means by which to introduce an element of competition into this loss making environment. The first involves the use of competitive tendering and requires the local authority to stipulate particular service requirements for the routes it intends providing a subsidy. The practice then involves bus operators competing for the licences to operate the subsidised routes. Selection is usually made on the basis of which company requires the least subsidy to provide the specified service.

The alternative to competitive tendering involves the full scale deregulation of the bus industry. This has been the approach advocated by Beesley and Glaister (1985) and contrasts strongly with the views of Gwilliam et al. (1985), who favour competitive tendering. The former however have argued that competitive tendering can only be effective if an industry is already deregulated. At the centre of this debate is the question of how to take proper account of the needs of the transport disadvantaged. The provision of an adequate level of public transport is regarded generally as a fundamental social requirement. Obtaining a planned, properly coordinated, integrated and reliable operation is at the core of the case put by Gwilliam et al. Deregulation is regarded as too drastic a step with the operators becoming the main arbiters in determining how the public interest is to be served.

The need to provide a stable supply of public transport services could not be guaranteed under full scale deregulation.

Local stage carriage services in England and Wales, other than in London, were deregulated in 1985. As in the airline industry, a considerable amount of restructuring has followed, with many observers estimating that this process will continue well into the 1990's.[9] In the first two years following the lifting of economic constraints bus mileage increased by 14%, whilst the number of passenger trips fell by 5.5%. Greater efficiency had the effect of reducing operating costs by some 6% over the same period, but as Robinson (1989) remarks..'..reduced loadings went a long way to wipe out the benefit of savings in operating costs..'. The decline in patronage is attributed to a number of factors, but of special concern given the nature of the business is the degree of confusion generated by deregulation in terms of the many changes to services that resulted. On the positive side marketing is far less stultified than it was and in many instances passengers have a wider choice of products than previously. In certain geographical locations the quality of service has also improved.

Growing concentration is also a feature of the deregulated bus industry. For example, of the original 72 subsidiaries of the National Bus Company, one third are now controlled by four corporations. This trend is expected by observers of the industry to continue, with between five to ten operators predicted to remain by the mid-1990s.[10] Despite the cited efficiency objective it would appear that the primary concern of bus deregulation was to reduce the level of operating subsidy. In this regard at least some success has been apparent, as by 1987/8 some 83% of all mileage was being operated commercially.[11]

A.4.4 Television and Radio

The approach favoured for commercial television and radio has involved the use of franchising. Limiting the number of television and radio channels has been necessitated firstly by the need to protect the British Broadcasting Corporation (BBC) and secondly by government desires to control the use of wavebands. Given these constraints the number of franchises available has been strictly limited, more especially in the case of television. Introducing an element of competition into this heavily controlled market has posed a considerable problem. Demsetz (1968), in an attempt to overcome this question in natural monopolies, advocated the use of franchising the right to be sole supplier in such a market, with interested parties being allowed to compete for an operating licence. By limiting the time that a licence was operative competitive pressure could be exerted and maintained. Rather than simply granting a franchise to the highest bidder, which, given public interest considerations could be inappropriate, it would be perfectly feasible for the franchising authority to determine an alternative goal, such as the lowest price to be charged to consumers.[12]

The viability of this approach depends critically on there being a number of interested bidders. Assuming, however, the existence of a sufficient number of potential rivals, in the absence of collusion and given a ready availability of input factors, price could be expected to be determined at a competitive level in the bidding market. Thus, as Demsetz (1968) has argued the requirement that regulatory authorities determine price could be dispensed with. This outcome, however, presupposes that franchises can be transferred in a 'frictionless' way, as Williamson (1976) has argued. Long lived assets are particularly problematical in this regard, as are matters relating to the acquisition of skill and knowledge by the workforce. Williamson's view[13] was that the mechanics of the transference process had been assumed away by Demsetz and Posner (1972), in their strong advocacy of franchising in preference to regulation. It may well be the case that once a firm has established itself as the holder of a franchise, rival firms will be at a relative disadvantage when the bidding recommences. If the..'..original winners of the bidding competition realise non-trivial advantages in informational and informal organisational respects during contract execution, bidding parity at the contract renewal interval can no longer be presumed.'[14] To minimise the likelihood of this occurring would necessitate careful monitoring and possible market intervention by the franchising authority. The net result would tend to bear an uncanny resemblance to regulation.

A further problem with franchised monopoly is that the firm once selected has little or no incentive to reduce cost.[15] Under such a regime the franchising authority ideally requires the use of a benchmark in order to be able to make reasonable judgements about the appropriate level of cost that a firm might be expected to incur in producing a particular service. Finding an acceptable candidate for comparison purposes is itself highly problematical. Schmalensee (1979) makes the point that it is inadvisable to contrast state-owned utilities with those in private ownership because of possible differences in attitude towards efficiency. In order to provide guidance to franchising authorities of attainable cost levels Schleifer (1985) proposes comparison between regulated firms possessing a high degree of similarity. He quotes the example of Medicare and its system of reimbursing hospitals, which is based on a comparison of incurred unit costs from treating patients within the same diagnostically related group.

A.4.5 Summary

In the case of franchising overall it would appear that the minutiae associated with individual markets in many instances conspire to confound the hope that it could provide an easy to administer and less costly alternative to regulation. Williamson (1976), for one however, has considered that local service airlines in the US would provide a good candidate for a franchising system. Such a system would appear to offer some useful possibilities for Europe, given its many advantages over both full scale deregulation and the tight form of economic regulation formally used. This issue is explored in detail in chapters 8 and 9.

Notes

1. Carried out by both the Office of Fair Trading and the Monopolies & Mergers Commission.
2. For example, the investigation into the Sealink/Townsend Thoresen duopoly of the short sea cross-Channel ferry trade carried out by the Monopolies and Mergers Commission.
3. Iain Vallance, British Telecom Chairman, 5th Annual General Meeting, July 1989.
4. To help overcome the problem of natural monopoly governments had taken industries into public ownership.
5. 1981 Telecommunications Act.
6. Littlechild, S. (1983), Regulation of British Telecommunications Profitability, HMSO, London.
7. OFTEL has scrutinised BT's pricing behaviour much more vigorously than was required under the RPI - X mechanism. As regards BT's rival Mercury, the regulatory body has acted to promote a competitive environment. The quality of BT's services have also been closely monitored by OFTEL.
8. Kay, J. A. & Vickers, J. S. (1988), 'Regulatory Reform in Britain', Economic Policy, October, p. 294.
9. Robinson, D. (1989), 'Where will it all end?', Transport, September, p. 197.
10. Robinson, D. (1989), supra note 9, p. 198.
11. Robinson, D. (1989), supra note 9, p. 197.
12. This particular method is generally referred to as the Chadwick-Demsetz proposal.

13. Williamson, O. E. (1976), 'Franchising Bidding for Natural Monopolies - In General and With Respect to CATV', Bell Journal of Economics, Spring, pp. 73-104.
14. Williamson, O. E. (1976), supra note 13, p. 89.
15. Assuming cost of service terms, with prices being adjusted periodically to reflect changes in the cost of providing the service.

Bibliography

Beesley, M. & Glaister, S. (1985), 'Deregulating the Bus Industry in Britain - A Response', Transport Reviews, Vol. 5.

Demsetz, H. (1968), 'Why Regulate Utilities?', Journal of Law and Economics, 1968, pp. 55-65.

Gwilliam, K. M., Nash, C. A. & Mackie, P. J. (1985), 'Deregulating the Bus Industry in Britain - The Case Against', Transport Reviews, Vol. 5.

Kay, J. A. & Vickers, J. S. (1988), 'Regulatory Reform in Britain', Economic Policy, October, p. 292.

Posner, R. A. (1972), 'The Appropriate Scope of Regulation in the Cable Television Industry', Bell Journal of Economics and Management Science, Spring, pp. 98-129.

Robinson, D. (1989), 'Where will it all end?', Transport, September, p. 197.

Schmalensee, R. (1979), The Control of Natural Monopoly, Heath, Lexington.

Shleifer, A. (1985), 'A Theory of Yardstick Competition', Rand Journal of Economics, Vol. 16, No. 3, Autumn, pp. 319-27.

Williamson, O. E. (1976), 'Franchising Bidding for Natural Monopolies - In General and With Respect to CATV', Bell Journal of Economics, Spring, pp. 73-104.

Appendix 5   Directory of West European Scheduled Passenger Carriers

Aer Lingus, the state-owned Irish flag carrier, operates a network of European services from its Dublin base. A small number of transatlantic routes are also provided. Liberalisation has enabled the carrier to operate a number of 'fifth freedom' routes from the UK to continental Europe. A fleet of 18 jet aircraft is currently operated.

Aer Lingus Commuter, an Aer Lingus subsidiary formed in 1984, operates a network of routes within Ireland and to the UK. A fleet of ten commuter aircraft is operated.

Air Dolomiti, an Italian regional carrier, was formed in 1991. A fleet of three commuter aircraft is currently operated.

Air Engiadina, a Swiss regional carrier, operates a network of inter-European services using a fleet of three commuter aircraft.

Air Exel Commuter, a Dutch regional carrier founded in 1991, operates services from Maastrict to Amsterdam and London using a fleet of three aircraft.

Air Europe ceased operations in 1991. The airline started life in 1979 as the charter subsidiary of Intasun, a UK based inclusive tour company. A transition to scheduled services was commenced in 1985. By 1990 a sizeable network of services had been established from Gatwick to European destinations. A key feature of the company's philosophy involved the undercutting of rivals' fares. Subsidiary airlines were established in Italy, Norway and Spain as part of the parent company's aim to develop services throughout Europe. A coincidence of rapid fleet and route expansion with a major economic recession in the UK sealed the fate of one of the most significant catalysts in what had been a comparatively stultified inter-European airline market.

Air France, the state-owned flag carrier, acquired a 35% shareholding in Sabena in 1992. The company had consolidated its position considerably in 1990 when it acquired controlling interests in Air Inter and UTA. Most recently the carrier has sold its stake in CSA, the Czech flag carrier. An extensive worldwide network of services is operated involving a fleet of some 160 aircraft and 42,000 staff. The carrier has formed a major alliance with Lufthansa.

Air Inter, the French domestic carrier, is now part of the Air France Group of companies. An extensive network of predominantly domestic services is operated involving a fleet of 65 jet aircraft and 11,000 staff.

Air Littoral, the French regional carrier based at Montpellier, operates a network of domestic and inter-European routes. KLM sold its 35% shareholding in the airline in 1993 to Euralair. A fleet of 17 aircraft is operated.

Air Nordic, a Swedish regional carrier, operates a network of services within Scandanavia using a fleet of five commuter aircraft.

Air UK operates a large domestic route network and serves Amsterdam from eight UK regional airports. Most recently the carrier has introduced a number of inter-European services from London's newly developed third airport at Stansted. KLM acquired a 15% shareholding in the airline in 1987. A fleet of 28 aircraft is operated.

Alitalia, the Italian state-owned flag carrier, operates a large international and domestic route network. The domestic airline ATI is a wholly owned subsidiary. The company employs 29,000 staff and operates a fleet of 110 jet aircraft.

AOM French A/l is the name adopted by the merged French airlines Air Outre Mer and Minerve. The latter carrier was established as a charter operator in 1975 concentrating mostly on long haul inclusive tour services. Air Outre Mer was formed in 1987 to operate scheduled services to the Caribbean and Reunion in the Indian Ocean. A fleet of twelve jet aircraft is now operated.

ATI, the Italian domestic carrier, is a fully owned subsidiary of Alitalia. An extensive network of domestic routes is operated using a fleet of 40 jet aircraft.

Aurigny, a UK domestic carrier, operates a network of services to the Channel islands using a fleet of ten commuter aircraft.

Austrian, the partly state-owned flag carrier, in addition to operating an extensive network of inter-European routes serves the Far and Middle East, North Africa and the USA. Swissair has a 10% shareholding in the airline. A staff of 4,600 are employed and a fleet of 24 jet aircraft operated.

Austrian Air Services, the wholly owned subsidiary of Austrian, operates a route network of domestic and regional commuter services. A fleet of seven aircraft is operated.

Aviaco, a subsidiary of Iberia, operates a large network of domestic services. The company also serves the Balearic and Canary Islands. The flag carrier has a 33% shareholding in the airline. A fleet of 31 aircraft is operated.

Avianova, the Italian regional carrier owned by ATI, operates a network of domestic and inter-European services. A fleet of eleven aircraft is operated.

BASE Business A/l, a Dutch regional carrier, operates a network of inter-European services using a fleet of three commuter aircraft.

Binter Canarias, a subsidiary of Iberia, operates a network of services in the Canary Islands. The company commenced operations in 1989 and now has a fleet of ten aircraft.

Binter Mediterranea, a subsidiary of Iberia, operates a network of services in the Balearic Islands and to the Spanish mainland. Services began in 1991 using a fleet of five commuter aircraft.

Braathens operates a large network of domestic services in Norway. The carrier, which was established in 1946, is also heavily engaged in charter work. The airline introduced a small number of international routes to Sweden and the UK in 1991. A fleet of 30 jet aircraft is currently in operation.

Brit Air, a French regional carrier, operates a network of domestic and inter-European services from Brittany and Normandy. The airline also operates on behalf of Air France and Air Inter. Founded in 1973, the company now operates a fleet of 20 aircraft.

British A/w, the privately owned flag carrier, has acquired shareholdings in a number of airlines, including Qantas (25%) and USAir (25%). Currently the most successful major carrier in Europe, it provides a worldwide network of services using a fleet of over 210 aircraft. In 1988 the airline acquired and absorbed British Caledonian. Dan-Air's scheduled operations were acquired in 1992. Charter carrier Caledonian is a fully owned subsidiary. An attempt to establish a jointly owned holding company with KLM foundered in 1992.

195

British Midland operates a large network of domestic and inter-European services. The airline is owned by Airlines of Britain Holdings in which SAS has a 35% shareholding. Loganair and Manx are also owned by the holding company. A fleet of 28 aircraft is currently operated.

Brymon Aviation, a regional carrier based at Plymouth, is a fully owned subsidiary of British Airways. The airline was owned until 1993 by The Plimsoll Line, in which British Airways and Maersk each had a 40% shareholding. A network of domestic and inter-European services are operated from Bristol and Plymouth using a fleet of ten commuter aircraft.

Business Air, a UK regional carrier, operates a network of inter-European and domestic services using a fleet of eight aircraft.

Cimber Air, a Danish regional carrier, operates a network of domestic and inter-European services. A fleet of ten aircraft is currently in use.

Cityflyer Express, a UK regional carrier, operates a network of inter-European services. The airline, which is based at Gatwick, operates its services using the brand name British Airways Express. A fleet of eight commuter aircraft is currently in use.

Cityjet, an Irish regional carrier, operates a service from Dublin to London City airport under the Vigin Atlantic brand name. A fleet of three jet aircraft is operated.

Contactair, a German charter carrier, operates a number of scheduled services on behalf of Lufthansa CityLine. The airline has a fleet of ten aircraft.

Conti-flug, a German regional carrier, operates a number of inter-European services from its Berlin base.

Corse Mediterranee, a regional carrier based in Corsica, operates a network of services to France and Italy. The airline was formed in 1989 and now operates a fleet of ten aircraft. Several of the company's services to the French mainland are operated in conjunction with Air France and Air Inter.

Crossair, the Swiss regional carrier, is a subsidiary of Swissair. A large network of domestic and inter-European services is operated. The airline besides operating its own flights provides services on behalf of its parent company. A fleet of 33 aircraft are used.

Dan-Air, a UK regional airline, ceased operating in November 1992. Its large network of domestic and inter-European routes were acquired by British Airways. The carrier also had been a major provider of inclusive tour charter services.

Delta AT, a Belgian regional carrier, is a subsidiary of Sabena. A network of inter-European services is operated. A fleet of 17 aircraft is currently used.

Deutsche BA, formerly known as Delta Air, is a German regional carrier. A 49% shareholding in the company was acquired by British Airways in 1992. Previously operating with a fleet of ten commuter aircraft, the airline has been re-equipped with jets.

EuroAir, a partially owned subsidiary of TAP - Air Portugal, was formerly known as LAR. The airline is currently operating a network of domestic services using . A fleet of three aircraft.

EuroBerlin, a carrier set up by Air France and Lufthansa to provide services from Berlin, is expected to cease operating by the end of 1994.

Eurowings, is the name adopted by the merged German regional carriers NFD and RFG. A network of domestic and inter-European services is operated using a fleet of 27 commuter aircraft.

Flexair, a Dutch regional carrier established in 1989, operates a service from Rotterdam to London City airport.

Gill Air is a UK domestic carrier based at Newcastle. A fleet of twelve commuter aircraft is currently operated.

Golden Air, a Swedish domestic carrier, is a subsidiary of Skyways. A fleet of four commuter aircraft is operated.

Hamburg A/l, a German regional carrier, operates a network of domestic and inter-European services. The company was formed in 1988 and now uses a fleet of seven commuter aircraft.

Holmstroem Air, a Swedish domestic carrier, operates a network of services using a fleet of six commuter aircraft.

197

Iberia, the state-owned Spanish flag carrier, operates a worldwide network of services. The carrier has acquired shareholdings in a number of South American airlines. Aviaco, Binter Canarias, Binter Mediterranea and VIVA Air are subsidiaries. A staff of 26,000 are employed and a fleet of 100 aircraft operated.

Interot A/w, a German domestic carrier, was formed in 1988. A network of services is operated from Augsberg using a fleet of four commuter aircraft.

Jersey European, a UK based carrier, operates a large network of mainly domestic services. A fleet of 15 aircraft is currently in use.

KLM, the Dutch flag carrier, operates a worldwide network of services. Formed in 1920, the company is now the oldest airline in existence. Shareholdings are held in a number of other carriers: Air UK (15%), KLM Cityhopper (100%), Martinair (34%), Northwest (20%) and Transavia (80%). Attempts to form a joint company with British Airways in 1991/2 failed to reach fruition. A fleet of 68 jet aircraft is currently operated.

KLM Cityhopper, the fully owned regional subsidiary of KLM, operates a network of domestic and inter-European services. Formerly known as NLM Cityhopper, the carrier took over the interests of Netherlines in 1988 and assumed its present name a year later. A fleet of 26 aircraft is currently operated.

Lauda Air, founded in 1979 as a charter carrier by the racing driver Niki Lauda, operates a network of services within Europe and to Australia, the Far East and USA. Lufthansa has a 26.5% shareholding in the airline through its charter subsidiary Condor. A fleet of eight aircraft is currently operated.

Loganair, a subsidiary of Airlines of Britain Holdings in which SAS has a 35% shareholding, operates an extensive network of services within Scotland. A fleet of thirteen commuter aircraft is currently used.

Lufthansa, the partially state-owned German flag carrier, operates a large worldwide network of services. The interests of the former East German carrier Interflug were acquired on reunification. The airline has two fully owned subsidiaries, Lufthansa CityLine and the charter carrier Condor. Major alliances have been formed with Air France and United. A staff of 45,000 are currently employed and a fleet of 200 aircraft operated.

Lufthansa Cityline, a fully owned subsidiary of Lufthansa, was formerly known as DLT. A network of domestic and inter-European services is operated. The airline currently has a fleet of 38 aircraft.

Luxair, the partially state-owned national airline of Luxemburg in which Lufthansa has a 13% shareholding, operates a network of inter-European services. A staff of 1,100 is currently employed and a fleet of twelve aircraft operated.

Maersk Air, the diversified Danish regional carrier, operates a network of domestic and inter-European services. In 1988 the airline acquired a 40% shareholding in The Plimsoll Line, of which Birmingham European and Brymon were until 1993 fully owned subsidiaries. A fleet of 26 aircraft is currently operated.

Maersk Air UK, a wholly owned subsidiary of Maersk Air, was known until 1992 as Birmingham European Airways. The carrier had been owned by The Plimsoll Line in which British Airways and Maersk each had a 40% shareholding. The airline was merged with Brymon in November 1992 adopting the name Brymon European. A year later the company was demerged with each parent carrier acquiring full control of its associate airline. Originally formed in 1983 to operate a network of inter-European services from Birmingham, the airline was purchased by The Plimsoll Line in 1988. A fleet of nine aircraft is currently operated.

Malmo Aviation, formerly known as CityAir Scandanavia, operates a small network of inter-European routes from its base at Malmo.

Manx, a subsidiary of Airlines of Britain Holdings in which SAS is a 35% shareholder, operates a network of domestic and inter-European services. British Midland and Loganair are sister companies of the airline. A fleet of 23 aircraft is currently in operation.

Martinair Holland, a subsidiary of KLM, operates a network of services from Amsterdam to Canada, the Caribbean and the USA. The carrier is also heavily engaged in charter work. A fleet of twelve aircraft is currently in operation.

Meridiana, known as Alisarda until 1991, is an Italian regional carrier based in Sardinia. A network of domestic and inter-European services are operated using a fleet of 18 jet aircraft.

Muk Air, a Danish regional carrier, operates services within Scandanavia using a fleet of seven commuter aircraft.

Olympic, the state-owned Greek flag carrier, operates a large network of domestic and international services. Olympic Aviation is a fully owned subsidiary. A fleet of 31 aircraft is currently operated.

Olympic Aviation, the Greek domestic carrier, is a fully owned subsidiary of Olympic. A fleet of 21 commuter aircraft is currently in operation.

Portugalia, a privately owned Portuguese carrier formed in 1989, operates a network of domestic services. The airline has been seeking to obtain licences for international operations. A fleet of four jet aircraft is currently operated.

Regional A/l, a French regional carrier, operates a large network of domestic and inter-European services. The company was formed in 1992 by the merger of Air Vendee and Airlec. A fleet of 17 commuter aircraft is currently in operation.

Rheintalflug, an Austrian regional carrier, operates a fleet of three commuter aircraft. The airline operates a number of services on behalf of Austrian Airlines.

Ryanair operates a network of services between Ireland and the UK. Commencing operations in 1986, the airline has had a profound effect on reducing fares on Irish Sea routes. A fleet of eight jet aircraft is currently in use.

Sabena, the Belgian flag carrier, operates a worldwide network of services. In 1992 Air France acquired a 35% shareholding in the airline. Earlier attempts by British Airways and KLM to establish links with the company were prevented by the European Commission. The airline has two subsidiaries: charter carrier Sobelair (100% owned) and regional operator Delta Air Transport (79% owned). A fleet of 33 jet aircraft is currently operated.

SAS, the partially state-owned flag carrier of Denmark, Norway and Sweden, operates an extensive worldwide network of services. The airline was the first in Europe to develop alliances with carriers around the globe. All Nippon, Thai and Varig are among the carriers with which SAS has formed collaborative ventures. In 1988 the company acquired a 10% equity interest in Texas Air Corporation, the then owners of Continental, which has since been disposed of. A 25% shareholding purchased in Airlines of Britain Holdings, parent company of British Midland, has since been raised to 35%. Subsidiaries of the airline include: Greenlandair (50% owned), SAS Commuter (100% owned) and Wideroe (22% owned). The company currently employs a staff of 34,000 and operates a fleet of 130 aircraft.

SAS Commuter, a fully owned subsidiary of SAS, operates a large network of routes mainly within Scandinavia. Formed in 1989, the airline currently operates a fleet of 30 aircraft.

Skyways, the Swedish domestic carrier formally known as *Avia*, operates a network of commuter services from its base at Norrkoping. Salair, another Swedish airline, was acquired in 1991. A fleet of eight aircraft is operated.

South East European, a Greek carrier, operates a scheduled service from Athens to London under the Virgin Atlantic brand name. A number of domestic services also are operated.

Swissair, the privately owned Swiss flag carrier, operates a large worldwide network of services. A number of shareholdings are held in other carriers: Austrian (10%), Balair/CTA (57%), Crossair (56%), Delta (6%) and Singapore (5%). The latter two named companies and Swissair have formed major alliances with each other. A staff of 17,000 is currently employed and a fleet of 61 jet aircraft operated.

TAP - Air Portugal, the state-owned flag carrier, operates a large network of routes throughout Europe and to Africa and North and South America. Regional airline EuroAir is a subsidiary of the company. A fleet of 38 aircraft is currently operated.

TAS A/w, an Italian carrier based in Milan, operates inter-European and domestic services. A fleet of two jet aircraft is operated.

TAT European, a French regional carrier, operates a large network of domestic and inter-European services. A 50% shareholding in the company was acquired by British Airways in 1993. A fleet of 60 aircraft is currently used.

Transwede, the Swedish regional carrier, operates a small network of domestic and inter-European services. Formerly concentrating on the provision of charter flights, the airline has developed a network of scheduled services. A fleet of twelve jet aircraft is currently in operation.

Tyrolean, an Austrian regional carrier based at Innsbruck, operates a network of domestic and inter-European services. A fleet of eighteen commuter aircraft is currently operated.

Virgin Atlantic, the privately owned UK carrier, operates a network of long haul international services. Founded in 1984 by Richard Branson, the company now has a fleet of twelve aircraft. Cityjet and South East European operate services within Europe using the Virgin brand name.

VIVA Air, a subsidiary of Iberia, operates a network of inter-European services. Formed in 1988 to operate charter flights, the company began operating scheduled services in 1991. A fleet of nine aircraft is currently used.

VLM, a Belgian regional carrier, began operating services in 1993 from Antwerp. A fleet of three aircraft is operated.

WDL, a German regional carrier, operates services on behalf of Lufthansa CityLine using a fleet of seven commuter aircraft.

Wideroe, a Norwegian domestic carrier, operates a large network of services. In 1991 the airline acquired Norsk Air, which it continues to operate as a separate venture. Braathens and SAS have shareholdings in Wideroe. A fleet of 26 commuter aircraft is currently operated.

Wideroe Norsk-Air, a wholly owned subsidiary of the Norwegian domestic carrier Wideroe, operates a small network of domestic and inter-European services. A fleet of three commuter aircraft is currently used.

Index

References from Notes are indicated by 'n' after the page number